Advanced
BUSINESS STUDIES
REVISION HANDBOOK

Andrew Gillespie

Oxford University Press

Oxford University Press, Great Clarendon Street, Oxford OX2 6DP

Oxford New York
Athens Auckland Bangkok Bogota Bombay
Buenos Aires Calcutta Cape town Dar es Salaam Delhi
Florence Hong Kong Istanbul Karachi
Kuala Lumpur Madras Madrid Melbourne
Mexico City Nairobi Paris Singapore
Taipei Tokyo Toronto

and associated companies in
Berlin Ibadan

Oxford is a trade mark of Oxford University Press

First published 1996

ISBN 0 19 832791 9 (Student's edition)
      0 19 832810 9 (Bookshop edition)

Typesetting, design and illustration by Hardlines, Charlbury, Oxford
Printed in Great Britain

CONTENTS

Answering business studies questions

Business Studies is a skills based subject which tests students' ability to use their knowledge.

There are four basic skills:

Level One	Description/Identification	Lowest level skill
Level Two	Explanation	
Level Three	Analysis	
Level Four	Evaluation	Highest level skill

To gain the highest grades, candidates must show evidence of the higher skills.

How to answer questions

Example question:

What determines the price of a product?

Example answer: _+ what competition doing,_
what is product, what is advertising needed which will increase costs & who will bear them consumers of co.

- The price of a product is influenced by the costs.

  candidate identifies a factor - level one

- This is because firms have to charge a price which is greater than costs to make a profit.

  candidate explains why cost is important - level two

- Profit is needed to reward the owners and to invest in the firm.   _- & shareholders / stake-holders_

  candidate develops point about profit - higher level two

- However in the short run a firm may sell a product at a loss. This may be to gain market share or because the product is still at the introduction phase and has high research and launch costs.

  candidate analyses the importance of covering costs - level three

- Overall it depends on whether we are considering a short or long term pricing policy. Firms may be willing to make a loss in the short run (for example in a price war) in order to ensure long term profits. It will also depend on the objectives of the firm. Some public sector organisations, for example, may simply try to cover costs.

  candidate begins to weigh up factors - level four

Key words/phrases

The following words and phrases are often useful when answering questions:

BECAUSE, THEREFORE - these are helpful when you want to explain a point.

HOWEVER, ON THE OTHER HAND - these are useful for analysis

ON BALANCE, OVERALL, IT DEPENDS, IN THESE CIRCUMSTANCES IT IS LESS LIKELY - these can be used when evaluating.

Example

Question: Should firms train their employees?

Answer:
By training their employees firms may be able to increase their profits BECAUSE trained staff are likely to be more productive and make less mistakes. _motivation_ Employees might also be more motivated BECAUSE they might be able to undertake more interesting work and BECAUSE managers are showing that they value their staff (which can satisfy their esteem needs). HOWEVER training costs money and is not always successful. It can also lead to a loss of production whilst staff are being trained.

OVERALL, management will have to weigh up the potential benefits against the costs. If, for example, the firm has the necessary resources, the training is relatively cheap and is likely to lead to significant increases in productivity and profitability the firm likely to invest in it. If, ON THE OTHER HAND, the firm lacks the necessary finance and staff already have the skills required then training is LESS LIKELY.

Key types of questions:

Key types of questions:	Responses should:
Identify/state/describe...	make a point
Explain/outline...	make a point and develop it
Discuss...	present two sides of the debate
Examine/assess/analyse...	make a point and develop fully with some questioning of it
Critically assess/to what extent...	explain both sides and evaluate

Don't be certain

Candidates should always avoid being too definite in their answers. Words such as 'will' and 'must' should be avoided and replaced by words and phrases such as 'might', 'may', 'could' and 'it is possible that'.

Example 1:

"If interest rates increase a firm's profits will fall". This is not true. A better answer would be: "If interest rates increase a firm's profits might fall".

.·. imports = cheaper
exports
but if liquidator our exports = more expensives
profit ↑.

Example 2:

"In a recession all firms sell less." Not true. "In a recession some firms sell less." _necessities will still have to be bought._

Example 3:

"In a monopoly market a firm will increase its prices." Not necessarily. "In a monopoly market a firm may be able to increase its price."

Nothing is definite. Organisations and managers are different. They do not all do the same thing or react in the same way. Some might do A. Others may do B. Answers should stress that there are a variety of responses to any situation.

less people will invest on the stock market, & more in banks.

Evaluation is the key skill for a Grade A

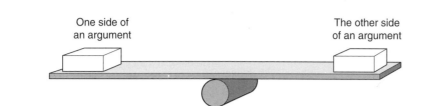

One side of an argument | The other side of an argument

Evaluation involves weighing up two sides of an argument.

To achieve the highest grades candidates must:

- identify relevant points on **both** sides of the argument. (level one)

- explain these points. (level two)

- analyse these points. (level three)

- evaluate them. (level four)

Level Four Answers

The key to producing Level Four answers is to highlight the fact that there is no single answer to a question - it always depends.

For example, when answering a question about how a firm might react to a change in, say, the external environment it is important to point out that the way in which a firm responds will depend on factors such as:

- The type of business - the objectives of a charity, for example, will differ from those of a public sector organisation or a private company. A small business operating in a local market will probably behave differently from a large multinational.

- The management —some managers are good, others are bad. Some react quickly to change, others react slowly, others do not react at all. Some managers will anticipate change (i.e be proactive); others will wait for it to happen (i.e be reactive)

- The state of the market - firms will behave differently in growing markets than in declining ones. A firm's behaviour will depend on whether it is in a competitive market or a monopoly.

- The state of the economy - a firm's behaviour will depend on whether it is in a recession or a boom; whether interest rates are high or low; whether the pound is weak or strong.

- Time - markets, consumers, employees, and suppliers in the 1990s are different from the 1980s and the 1970s, and will probably be different in the year 2000. Their attitudes, expectations and values will change. Just because something happens one year does not mean it will continue. Trends such as the growth of the 'green' consumer and the success of franchises in the 1990s will not necessarily continue into the next decade.

- Country - UK laws, attitudes, and markets differ from those in, say, Japan. What is allowed, accepted or encouraged here is not necessarily the case elsewhere.

Good answers present two sides of an argument and then weigh them up.

[handwritten margin notes:] era's. 6 answers as to why businesses react diff. Time, market, type of co, country, economy, management. IMPORTANT.

[handwritten numbers in margin:] 1, 2, 3, 4, 5, 6

Typical essay questions.

Question 1: Consider the effect of an increase in interest rates on a firm.

Answer:

Candidates need to discuss the way in which a firm might be affected (e.g. sales, production and employment levels) and then evaluate. In this case the effect depends on factors such as:

- how much have interest rates increased?
- how long will the rates remain high?
- what type of goods or services does the firm produce? Are these sensitive to interest rate changes?

If rates have increased significantly, have been high for a long time and the firm produces goods which are sensitive to interest rates (e.g. houses) the impact is likely to be greater than if rates have only just gone up by a small amount.

Question 2: "Autocratic management is dead." Critically assess this view.

Candidates should:

- briefly explain what is meant by autocratic management,
- explain why it might be thought to be dead e.g. employees' desire to be involved, to have greater responsibility, greater belief in democratic styles, success of democratic styles
- explain why autocratic management might be needed e.g. if there is limited time, a high degree of risk or staff are untrained
- evaluate; e.g. if staff are unwilling to take responsibility, there is a tight deadline, the company's culture is autocratic and the manager is reluctant to delegate the firm is more likely to be autocratic.

When answering essay questions candidates should avoid simply repeating their notes or the textbook. Good answers must refer to the specific question and rework notes and ideas accordingly.

Example:

To what extent is price the most important factor in marketing?

If candidates answer this question by listing the four P's of the marketing mix their mark will be very low indeed. A good answer would consider the other elements of the mix but in the context of when price is more important or less important.

For example, price might be more important when:

- the consumer has a low income (e.g. in a recession) and so shops around
- in a competitive market with many similar substitutes
- when goods are easily comparable

Price might be less important:

- in a boom
- for heavily branded goods
- in the growth stage of the life cycle
- if the good is patented
- if it is a speciality good

Overall, the importance of the price depends on factors such as:

- income levels
- the role of promotion
- where the good is distributed
- the nature of the market

Coursework

For most coursework assignments candidates must

- apply business studies theory
- show research skills
- show communication skills
- analyse a relevant business issue
- evaluate by showing a judgement of the issues involved

Candidates should check the assessment criteria before starting their research so they know what skills they must demonstrate and the relative weighting of the different skills.

Candidates should plan their coursework before gathering data to ensure their project will meet the set criteria e.g. they should plan how they are going to gather data, what theory will be covered.

Candidates should avoid descriptive projects - projects must show evidence of analysis.

Candidates should make sure:

- they can gather the data relatively easily
- the title is not too broad

Typically projects are:

i. problem solving e.g. should XYZ invest in new equipment?
ii. a comparison e.g. how do the recruitment methods of ABC compare with those of DEF Ltd?

Projects should contain:

- a title
- the name of the candidate
- an index
- an appropriate use of headings and sub headings
- an appropriate use of charts/graphs and tables
- a conclusion
- a list of source material

6 factors that will determine how firm copes in ❓ ways
type of co, market, economy, managers, time, country
3   4   2   5   6

Organisations

An organisation is a collection of people which exists to achieve collective goals and in which behaviour is controlled.

→(profit, < market share, to improve standards of living/health)

Organisations can be categorised by

- size   based on e.g. turnover, assets, number of employees
  no. of

- sector   private sector - owned by private individuals
              public sector - owned by the Government

- activity   primary   - directly related to natural resources (e.g. fishing, farming, mining)
              secondary - processing of materials e.g. manufacturing   *quaternary - information.*
              tertiary   - services e.g. banking

- legal form e.g. whether it is a company with a legal identity separate from its owners *∴ owners don't have liability.*

organisation - size, sector, activity, legal form.

Most of the income in the UK is increasingly generated by
the tertiary sector:

% of Gross Domestic Product (at factor cost)	1964	1993
PRIMARY	5.8	3.9
SECONDARY	40.8	28.4
TERTIARY	53.8	67.7

Source : CSO

decrease 1.9%
decrease 12.4%
↑13.9%

3.8
3.9
1.9
40.8
28.4
12.4
53.8
67.7
53.8
13.9

PRIMARY
TERTIARY — SECONDARY

1993

The majority of people in the UK are increasingly employed
in the tertiary sector:

% of total employment	1964	1993
PRIMARY - *∴ unemployment was ↑*	5.1	1.5
SECONDARY	46.9	25.2
TERTIARY	47.8	73.0
Total number employed	22,357,000	21,554,000

Source : CSO, National Income and Expenditure

-3.6%
-21.7%
+25.2
- total no ↓ ∴ ↑ in unemployment - esp since pop growth = ↑ since 1960's.

.1   46.9
.5   25.2
.6   21.7
73.0
47.8
25.2

PRIMARY
TERTIARY — SECONDARY

1993

All organisations transform inputs into outputs:

Transformation process:

| INPUTS e.g. people, raw materials, money, land | → | TRANSFORMATION PROCESS e.g. extracting, manufacturing, assembling, refining, adding, designing, mixing, combining | → | OUTPUTS e.g. finished goods and services |

m = ofits.

The aim of organisations is to generate outputs which have a
greater value than the inputs used up. Business organisations
generally value inputs and outputs in monetary terms ;

Business aim/objective.
therefore the aim is usually to generate a revenue which is
greater than the costs i.e. to make a profit.

Value added: the difference between the outputs and the
value of the bought in inputs. This is used to :
- reward employees (e.g. wages and salaries),
- reward owners (e.g. dividends) *(shareholders & stakeholders)*
- invest (retained profit)
- and pay tax.

ugh

Competitive advantage: an aspect of the firm's behaviour or
performance which gives it a competitive edge over its
competitors, e.g. it may be a lower cost producer, or have a
unique selling proposition (USP), such as being the only
company to deliver to your door the next day.

value added = difference between input costs & output costs co. react (6 diff factors) 1- type of co. 2, - managers 3, - market 4 - economy 5, Time 6 - country.

Decision making

Managing a business successfully involves effective decision making. When undertaking the decision making process a firm will:

1
Set objectives — e.g. short or long term profits, growth, customer satisfaction

↓

2
Gather information — market research

↓

3
Analyse information — e.g. investment appraisal, break-even analysis, ratio analysis

↓

4
Select a course of action — e.g. enter new market, buy another firm — Take over bid

↓

5
Implement — take action, do it

↓

6
Review — check to see if it is going according to plan

(↺ loops back to Set objectives)

Strategic decisions for long term
- long term, high risk
- difficult to reverse if wrong
- managers have often never made this type of decision before, e.g. what markets to enter

Tactical decisions for short term less of a risk - though still some risk.
- short term, easier to reverse
- managers have often made similar decisions before, e.g. what price to charge
- usually involve less resources

Objectives may include:

1 Survival — in the short run firms may have to sacrifice profit to survive, e.g. in a price war. Ensuring the firm is liquid is often a priority in the short run.

2 Profit — to reward owners, to invest into the business, as an indicator of success to attract investors

3 Growth — to gain economies of scale, and to gain market power

4 Customer satisfaction — to increase demand and lead to long term profits

5 Provide a service to the public — community spirit — consumers will look favourably on such competitors. e.g. public corporations, hospitals, libraries.

Constraints on decision making

Internal

Factors a firm can control, but which restrict its ability to achieve its objectives.

Finance - e.g. cashflow, ability to raise finance

Marketing - e.g. limited salesforce distribution

Human resources - e.g. numbers, skills, motivation, attitudes

Production - e.g. capacity, quality, flexibility

External

Factors beyond the immediate control of the firm, which restrict its ability to achieve its objectives.

Political factors - e.g. Government policy

Economic factors - state of economy

Social factors - e.g. social trends, demographics, attitudes

Technology - e.g. rate of charge

Management process

Management is about 'getting things done through others' (R. Stewart).
It involves deciding what has to be done and how to do it; and making sure the right decisions are implemented.

delegating - but must have faith in workforce before this can be done.

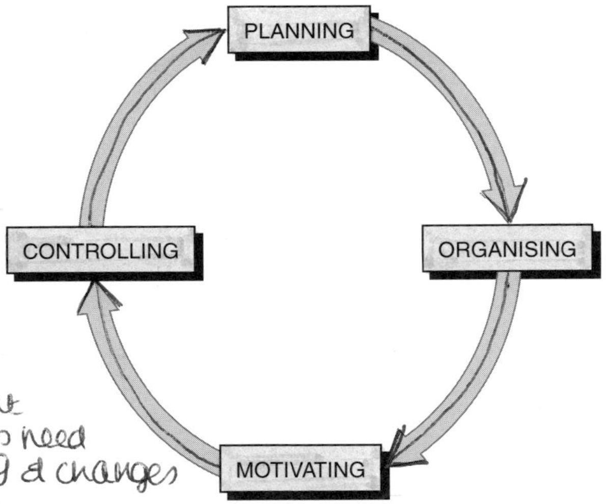

PLANNING
ORGANISING
MOTIVATING
CONTROLLING

Management is a dynamic process - it is ongoing and ever changing as the challenges, resources and constraints of a firm change.

Businesses are never static ∴ management team always need to be working & changes to fit in with consumer attitudes.

Management skills

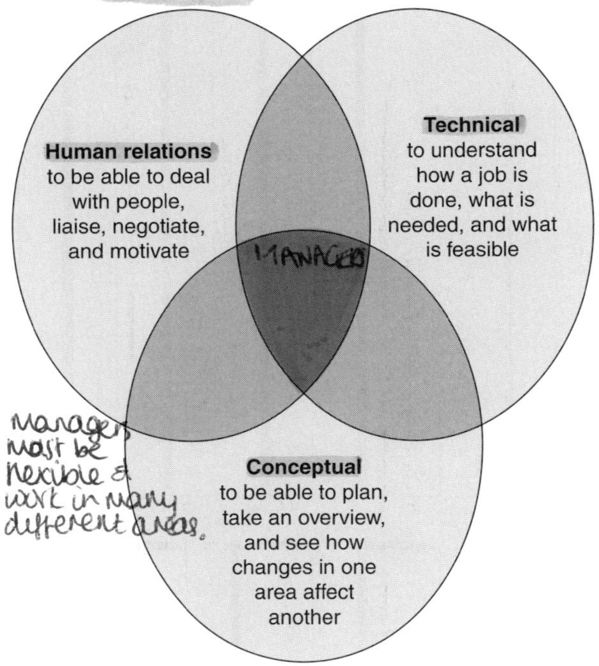

Human relations
to be able to deal with people, liaise, negotiate, and motivate
Technical
to understand how a job is done, what is needed, and what is feasible
Conceptual
to be able to plan, take an overview, and see how changes in one area affect another
MANAGER

Managers must be flexible & work in many different areas.

Management hierarchy

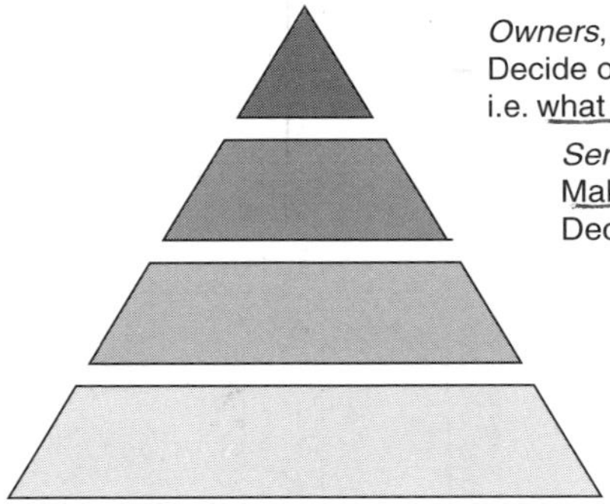

Owners, e.g. shareholders — only have power to decide if 51% of co. or more - less & have little say in running of co.
Decide overall mission of the organisation, i.e. what is there to achieve

Senior managers, e.g. Marketing Director
Make strategic decisions. ← long term decision
Decide how to achieve the objectives of the owners

Middle management, e.g. factory managers
Implement decisions of senior managers.
Decide the best ways of carrying out these plans — as they know employees - find a way to get most out of them in a productive way

First line/supervisory management, e.g. supervisors
Oversee operatives.
Ensure the orders of the middle management are carried out
responsibility for ensuring all goes to plan.

~~Owners~~ — Shareholders = - owners
- managers
- employees
- individuals
- financial institutions (insurance/pension schemes)
- foreign companies

Divorce between ownership and control: the managers who control the organisation day to day may have different objectives from the owners, e.g. the managers may want to invest to grow whereas the owners may want higher dividends, i.e. there may be a divorce between their objectives.

— gives everyone a goal to look towards

Mission statement: states the overall aims of the organisation and its values. The aim is to develop a common sense of purpose, e.g. the mission might be 'to be the world's best airline' or 'to protect and serve'.

Objectives: must be quantifiable and time specific, e.g. to increase sales by 20% over three years.

gives a sense of responsibility to all ∴ greater motivation & maybe greater productivity.

Management by objectives: managers agree objectives with employees. The result is that employees have clear goals. Progress can be reviewed at the next meeting.

— FW Taylor approach.

Scientific management: managers decide on the one best way of completing a task, train employees, and reward them for higher output. It assumes that managers are there to think, whereas employees are simply there to implement and are motivated by money. The scientific approach creates a system of rules and procedures for employees to follow. It leads to predictable, consistent results, but can be demotivating if employees wish to be involved and use their initiative. ← motivation = money, not promotion.

What if things go wrong?

Crisis management: describes how the managers prepare for and react to a sudden change, e.g. BSE scare about British beef, Perrier's reaction to discovery of imperfections in their water, the Stock Market crash of 1987, the exchange rate crisis of 1992, bombing of offices, sudden closure of supplier, or a strike.

Contingency planning: attempting to predict different scenarios and planning suitable strategies for each one.

usually if co. is successful, then money is put into contingency fund, for such a disaster.

Business formats 1

People set up a business because:
- they want to work for themselves (independence)
- they have been made redundant from their last job
- they cannot find another job
- they want to achieve something for themselves (self actualisation) — Maslow.
- it is a natural progression from a hobby or interest

sometimes ~~usually~~ people have ambitions, which they can't complete because of job & don't want to risk failure, job loss can be the impetous needed & ∴ they achieve their ambition & will work at it.

An entrepreneur is someone who:
- combines resources
- identifies opportunities
- takes risks
- makes decisions

usually will employ others to carry out what is wanted.
ie Richard Branson - Virgin
Anita Roddick - Body Shop.

To achieve the finance to set up a business, individuals often require a business plan. — *Banks look favourably on those who have thought upon such procedures.*

Business plan: a report showing plans of the business; often used to attract finance from investors. Businesses which put time and effort into their business plans, thinking about the competition and the financial consequences of their proposals, are more likely to be successful than those which do not.

The main elements of business plan include:

1. - a description of the business - What does it make? What service does it provide?

2. - a statement of its aims - what are the aims of the business in the short and long term?

3. - a marketing plan - e.g. Who needs the product/service? Why? What makes it different, i.e. what is its unique selling proposition (USP)? Who is the competition? What will the price be?

profit & loss & balance sheets can be window dressed, so therefore for a good business, a cash flow statement is necessary.

4. - a list of key personnel - details of who is setting up the business (background, experience)

5. - a projected profit and loss

6. - a projected balance sheet

7. - a projected cash flow statement

8. - details of the finance required - What will it be used for? What is the expected rate of return for investors?

See pg 43.

Sole trader — *not on stock market*
An individual who owns the business, e.g. a window cleaner, local shopkeeper, or hairdresser

motivation at being own boss.

Advantages
- can make decisions quickly
- keeps all the rewards
- easy to set up
- privacy of business affairs

In 1993 there were 3.6m businesses in the UK. 2.6m of these were sole traders or partnerships without employees.

Disadvantages
- limited sources of finance (e.g. own funds)
- unlimited liability, i.e. can lose personal assets
- often has limited managerial skills
- no one to share workload with
- no one to share ideas with

input is from one, ∴ perspective can be narrow & ambition not realistic (very pessimistic though.)

business can fail if ill.

must be able to do many things — can not specialise.

Partnership

Two or more people trading together 'carrying on business with a view to profit' (1890 Partnership Act).

A maximum of 20 partners is allowed, except for partnerships in the professions such as law and accountancy.

Advantages

- share resources/ideas

- can cover for each other, e.g. during holidays / illness.

- more sources of finance than sole trader

- partners can specialise, e.g. one may specialise in company law, another may focus on criminal law

Disadvantages

- usually unlimited liability

- limited sources of finance - not *shares on stockmarket*

- profits must be shared between partners

- slower decision making than sole trader

- If one partner dies, the partnership must be dissolved.

- what one partner says the rest *must follow (depends on Deed of Partnership though.)*

Deed of partnership: a legal document which forms a contract between the partners. It covers issues such as the division of profits, the dissolution (closure) of the partnership; the rights of each partner; the rules for taking on new partners.

Sleeping partner: invests in partnership but does not take part in day to day business; has limited liability. At least one partner must have unlimited liability. *(ie can lose personal assets.)*

Co-operative

A democratic organisation where all members have one vote. It's possible to have shareholders in a co-operative, but the shareholders have one vote each rather than one vote per share. This means no one member can easily dominate.

There are several types of co-operative, e.g.

a. **Worker co-operative:** organisation owned by employees. Employees should be motivated but can have problems managing themselves.

b. **Retail co-operative** set up to benefit consumers, e.g. the CO-OP. Surpluses distributed via lower prices.

Public sector organisations

Owned or directed by the Government.

Examples include the BBC, the Bank of England, the armed services, and local authority services such as schools, parks, museums, and libraries. Revenue often comes from the taxpayer as well as customers. Likely to have social objectives; not just be profit oriented

Non profit organisations, e.g. charities such as
Oxfam, sports clubs, or societies; non profit objectives; often have voluntary workers.

Business formats 2

If a co. goes ~~bankrupt~~ into liquidation, certain people receive their money 1st - & some won't get any money back.

Companies

A company has a separate legal identity from its owners. A company owns assets, and it can sue and be sued. A company is owned by shareholders. Shareholders have limited liability - i.e. they can lose the money they have invested in the business but not their personal assets.

control if 51%+

Forming a company

memorandum of association

includes:

1. name of company
2. company objectives
3. location of registered office

+

articles of association

internal rules of company

e.g. powers of directors, rights of shareholders, types of share

sent to the
Registrar of Companies
who sends back a
Certificate of incorporation

Private company (Ltd)

- must have 'Ltd' after its name
- restrictions can be placed on sale of shares *(Ltd)*
- not allowed listing on stock exchange *(diff to get finance - from friends/relations)*
- not allowed to advertise their shares *(another constraint)*
- usually smaller (although some are large e.g. Littlewoods)

v

Public company (Plc)

- must have PLC after its name
- can be quoted on Stock Exchange *finance (easier to get)*
- minimum £50,000 authorised share capital
- shareholders have right to sell their shares to whoever they want
- usually larger

All companies:
must produce a set of accounts for each shareholder; a copy of the accounts is kept at Companies House. The annual report and accounts must include: a balance sheet, profit and loss, a cash flow statement, a directors' report, and an auditor's report. The annual report of a PLC is more detailed than a Ltd's.

Being quoted on the Stock Exchange

- provides access to more investors
- raises the profile of the company, and attracts more media attention

but

- the process of becoming quoted (flotation) can be expensive and time consuming
- there is no control over the sale of shares by investors - this makes the PLC vulnerable to take-over *(hostile)*
- PLC's have to reveal more information than Ltd's

Some firms have become a PLC and then returned to being a Ltd e.g. Andrew Lloyd Webber's Really Useful Group, and Richard Branson with Virgin.

There are about 1m limited liability companies in Great Britain (excluding Northern Ireland).

'Flotation': process of becoming a PLC *(float on the stock exchange market.)*

To become a plc, i.e. to float, a company must:

- produce a prospectus giving details about the company, e.g. its activities and accounts
- meet the requirements of the Company Acts and the Stock Exchange

Five largest public companies in UK:	Market Capitalisation £m April 1996
1. British Petroleum	33,434
2. Shell	29,304
3. Glaxo Wellcome	27,752
4. HSBC	26,101
5. British Telecom	23,371 Source : Sunday Times 14/4/96

Shareholders elect
Directors who oversee
Managers

What is the value of a company?

Market capitalisation: market value of company; market price of shares x number of shares

Book value: value of company as stated in its accounts. *(can be window dressed)*

Directors - elected by shareholders; oversee managers to ensure they are working in the interests of the shareholders; the directors are the 'watchdogs' of the shareholders; the directors are responsible for the overall strategy of the company, subject to approval by the shareholders; their conditions of appointment and powers are stated in articles of association. Non executive directors are - part timers who have no day to day involvement (no executive powers) in the organisation

Company Secretary - company official with responsibility for maintaining a register of shareholders, notifying shareholders of annual general meeting, and preparing the company's annual returns. *annual general meetings = essential (legally)*

Cadbury Committee - reported on the role of directors. It recommended more non executive directors to keep an independent eye on the business. Public limited companies must state the extent to which they comply with the Cadbury Codes of Best Practice in their annual report.

Corporate governance - issue of who really controls companies, e.g. do the institutional investors exercise too much power? *(financial institutions = insurance co's / pension co's)*

Different types of shares

Ordinary shareholders
- have one vote per share
- can attend annual general meeting (AGM)
- are sent company accounts
- receive a dividend if one is paid
- can vote on directors

more risky, but benefits can be high

Preference shareholders
- have no vote
- receive a fixed dividend
- are paid in preference to ordinary shares but after loan repayments

Less risk, but will not benefit from 'good' years, though will be happier in 'bad' years.

Types of share capital:

Authorised: maximum value of shares which company can issue; listed in the articles of association.

Issued: amount of shares actually issued. The issued share capital cannot be greater than the authorised.

Called up share capital: face value of all the shares paid for by shareholders.

Owning other companies

Holding company: controls other companies but is not involved in their day to day running. *(∴ gets profits for owning)*

Subsidiary: B is a subsidiary of A if A has more than 50% of the shares in B or has a controlling interest.

A has 50%+ of B, so, B = subsidiary of A.

Associate company: B is an associate company of A if A has between 20 and 50% of the shares of B.

→ where A has sufficient control (in no. of shares) over B.

Stock exchange: market for shares; mainly second hand shares are traded i.e. shares which have already been issued by companies. In 1993 there were 1,927 UK and Irish companies with a full listing on the London Stock Exchange.

FTSE- FINANCIAL TIMES STOCK EXCHANGE.

FTSE- Financial Times Stock Exchange - an index of the share prices of the top 100 companies listed in the Financial Times. Its base is 1000.

FTSE 100 - PRICE INDEX

The price of a share is determined by:
- the number of issued shares – *if lots of shares* — *ie demand is low then price will be low.*
- the expected dividends *(more expensive if ↑ dividend)*
- stockbrokers' and analysts' reports - *expert advice.*
- the rates of return available elsewhere – *competition of other shares or ie if interest ↑ people may invest in banks for high interest rate & zero risk.*
- the present and expected profitability of the company

if future looks good – profits will be higher ∴ dividends higher so more people will want shares.

Ownership of shares in the UK

The main shareholders in the UK are financial institutions, such as pension funds, not individuals.

Individuals

Foreign

Other holders *(managers, owners, directors!)*

Non-financial enterprises *(charities?)*

Financial sector

incorporated body - co. with separate identity from owners.
unincorporated body - no distinction between co. & owners

Business formats 3

Franchises – *ie Body Shop. Individuals buy a 'name' & its products & profit stays with them.*
A franchisor sells the right to use/sell a product or service to a franchisee in return for a fixed fee and/or percentage of the turnover, for example: McDonald's, Unigate Dairies, Hertz, Kall Kwik

Why buy a franchise? – *low risk unless go to 'bad' area.*
- existing, established product; already known, therefore, cheaper market research and promotional costs
- may receive help and training from franchisor
- can share marketing costs, research findings, new product development costs
- lower start up costs

so name of Franchisor co. is not damaged.

Why sell a franchise?
- quicker growth; can cover a geographic area more quickly
- provides funds
- managers more motivated as they own the franchise

If franchise to wrong people, name of co. can be damaged, people may take liberties as they see it as their own shop.

ADVs→ managers already know ropes, will be highly motivated, won't be hostile.

Opposing = management buy ins where unrelated company buys into the company

Management buy outs MBO
Existing managers take over the company, e.g. Oxford Bus Company. Often companies are sold to managers when an organisation is 'unbundling' (i.e. getting back to its core business), or when a business is privatised. *or when retirement of family business, managers keep it going.*

Multinationals: Firms with production bases in more than one country; they may have locations around the world but have their headquarters in one country, e.g. BP, Shell,

Reasons for becoming multinational:
- to make use of resources abroad e.g. raw materials – *esp. when raw materials almost exhausted elsewhere.*
- to be closer to markets
- to avoid legislation in their own country which may prevent firms getting too big
- to gain tax advantages or grants from overseas governments → *Multinationals need good infrastructure and are prepared to pay*
- weakens domestic unions by spreading bases around the world

Why welcome a multinational?
- provides jobs *∴ improves economy.*
- pays taxes
- provides skills and management techniques
- provides goods and services
- reduces levels of imports

can improve infrastructure

knock on effects of having jobs→ high morale in country.

Why be suspicious?
- may not share skills or knowledge
- may not invest in country
- may not train locals
- may pressurise government
- may damage environment
- is footloose so can 'dump' country *whenever (though mayn't because public opinion would be hostile)*

Reaction should depend on: which multinational it is and the extent to which it will be or can be regulated.

Liquidation... turning assets into cash. Occurs when co. ceasing to trade in current form, probably to improve solvency. It assets are strong, then buyer can buy & carry on the running of the co. (receiver appoint to raise the cash.

Joint ventures/ strategic alliances
Companies work together on specific projects. They can share costs and profits, e.g. Ford and Mazda produce cars together.

∴ both projects

bankruptcy - indiv./unincorporated body may result (action) bankrupt when unable to settle liabilities - or act in a similar manner. Limited liability NOT applied to.

Closure of a business
1986 Insolvency Act: covers the options open to a company which is insolvent. An insolvent company may seek a voluntary agreement under which company and creditors agree to a scheme of reduced or delayed payments.

If this is not possible, a firm may ask for a bankruptcy court to appoint an 'administrator' to try to reorganise the company. If successful, the administrator returns the company to its management. If unsuccessful, the next stage is receivership - assets are sold to pay off secured creditors. If the company still cannot be saved, it may be 'wound up' - assets sold and proceeds distributed amongst its creditors.

If an individual is insolvent this is called 'bankruptcy'.

Why do firms fail?
- poor planning *(or just short term planning)*
- cashflow problems
- overtrading
- increased competition *→ external*
- decline of market *- fashions/ trends*
- failure to react to market trends *— internal*

Insolvency occurs when a firms external liabilities are greater than its assets - revealed through an inability to meet financial obligations. A business which continues to trade when insolvent is operating illegally.

Small firms

Small firms

The definition of a "small" firm varies. In the UK the Department of Trade has the following definitions:

- 'micro' - up to nine people

- 'small' - ten to ninety-nine people

- 'medium' - one hundred to four hundred and ninety-nine people

Other official definitions of small use a turnover of less than £1m or £500,000 as well as fewer than 200 or 500 employees.

The 1971 Bolton Committee concluded small firms had three main characteristics:

- relatively small share of the market

- managed by owners and part owners in a personalised way without a formal management structure

- not part of a larger organisation (e.g. not owned by another larger company)

Statistics

- small and medium-sized businesses account for about two thirds of private sector employment

- small companies account for nearly one quarter of gross domestic product ← *money produced within domestic market over a period ie 1 yr.* *value of countrys output*

- 97% of UK businesses have a turnover of less than £1m

- 78% of UK business have a turnover of less than £100,000

How do small firms survive?
- offer personal service
- serve niche markets
- have greater flexibility
- innovative
- *have more time to personalise products*

Why do governments like small firms?
- innovative
- create jobs
- fill niches
- provide competitions for larger firms
- sell abroad increasing exports

boost economy, but don't have much control within a country

All these should encourage the setting up of small firms.

- Alternative Investment Market - provides market for shares of smaller firms without as many regulations and expenses as a full listing on the Stock Exchange. (replaces Unlisted Securities Market USM)

- Loan Guarantee Scheme - government guarantees a proportion of a small firm's loan in return for a fee. Provides small firms with more opportunity to borrow.

- Information and advice - e.g. Training and Enterprise Councils. (TEC's)

- Business Start Up Scheme - provides financial help for unemployed individuals setting up new businesses (previously the Enterprise Allowance).

- Tax allowances - small firms pay a reduced rate of corporation tax.

Government help

- Enterprise Investment Scheme - Income tax relief for investors in small companies (previously the Business Expansion Scheme). → *tax*

- Enterprise Initiative grants for small companies employing less than 25 people in development areas. *enterprise zones, in areas where employment is lowest*

- Small Firms Merit Award for Research and Technology (SMART) - financial support for development of new technology with commercial potential for firms with less than 50 employees.

- Support for Products Under Research (SPUR) - funds for development of new products and processes for firms with less than 250 employees.

- Less government interference - in the 1980s and 1990s various schemes have been introduced to reduce government regulations and bureaucracy for small firms, e.g. the accounts small companies have to file are simpler than for larger companies. ↳ *red tape*

training loan. stock exchange.
for redundant
more of a hassle - easier scheme for redundant

Sources of advice for small firms include:
- Training and enterprise Councils (TECs)
- Local Chambers of Commerce

- Local Enterprise Agencies (LEAs)
- Business Links (brings together the services of, e.g. TECs, LEAs, and Chambers of Commerce in one location)

groups of business people in a town/city who gather together as a pressure group to look after the interests of local firms. work with TECs to improve training in area.

Growth

The size of a firm can be measured by, e.g. assets, employees, turnover.

A firm may be large using one indicator but small using another, e.g. the National Health Service has a large number of employees but a low turnover.

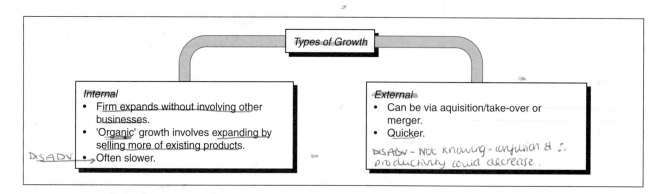

Types of Growth

Internal
- Firm expands without involving other businesses.
- 'Organic' growth involves expanding by selling more of existing products.
- *DISADV* → Often slower.

External
- Can be via aquisition/take-over or merger.
- Quicker.

DISADV - Not knowing = confusion & s. productivity could decrease.

Integration occurs when two or more firms join together - it might be through a merger or a take-over

Merger: mutual agreement between two or more companies to join together.

Why merge?
- Share resources
- Gain economies of scale
- Quick growth, *can monopolise (depending on account from monopolies & mergers commission)*

Problems merging
- Culture clash
- Government may prevent it if it forms a monopoly
- *who will be ultimate boss*
- *loss of jobs can occur.*

can be hostile & predatory - ie large amounts of shares bought up entitling owners to control co - can be done without co. being taken over realising.

Takeover: occurs when one firm gains control of another. It may be via a cash offer or a paper offer (offer shares in own company in return for shares in target company) or a combination of the two.

Trigger points:
- the attacker must inform the target company when it has 5% of its shares.
- when it has 15% of the victim's shares, the attacker must wait seven days to give the directors of the target company time to organise their defence
- when the attacker has 30% it is obliged to bid for the target company

Timetable: Once a firm makes a bid it has 60 days starting from the day formal documents go out in which to succeed. If bid fails, the attacker must wait at least a year before trying again.

Type of integration	Description	Possible reasons
Horizontal *same kind of co. ie Nestlé & Cadbury.*	same stage of same production process	market power, economies of scale
Vertical - *linked in same way, ie A = component of B*	different stage of same production process	control suppliers or outlets
Conglomerate - *completely different. periphery business.*	different production process	spread risks

bird's eye view

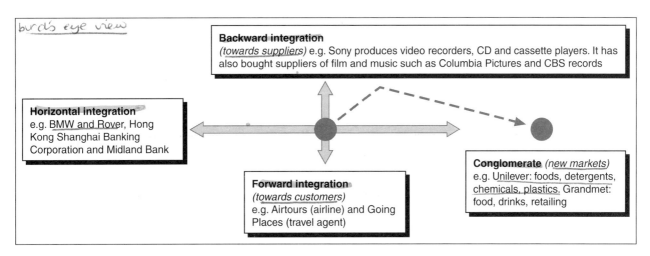

Horizontal integration
e.g. BMW and Rover, Hong Kong Shanghai Banking Corporation and Midland Bank

Backward integration
(*towards suppliers*) e.g. Sony produces video recorders, CD and cassette players. It has also bought suppliers of film and music such as Columbia Pictures and CBS records

Forward integration
(*towards customers*)
e.g. Airtours (airline) and Going Places (travel agent)

Conglomerate (*new markets*)
e.g. Unilever: foods, detergents, chemicals, plastics. Grandmet: food, drinks, retailing

Economies of scale

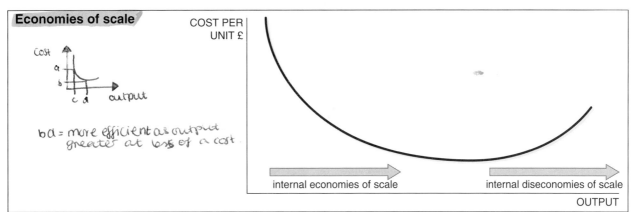

COST PER UNIT £

bd = more efficient as output greater at less of a cost.

internal economies of scale

internal diseconomies of scale

OUTPUT

Internal economies of scale
Cost advantage of producing on a larger scale. As output increases, cost per unit falls.

- Financial - cheaper borrowing as firm gets bigger and has more assets and collateral *∴ easier to borrow from banks...*
- Managerial - can employ specialists, number of managers will not grow at same rate as sales *∴ get more skill for money ∴ more efficiency a profitability*
- Technical - can use mass production techniques *(can be problems with this)*
- Purchasing - discounts for bulk buying, can negotiate better terms *← ie co-op.*
- Risk bearing economies - less risk as can diversify into different areas. *-though sometimes efficiency can be hindered.*

Diseconomies of scale
If firm gets too big the costs per unit may increase. This is due to problems with:

- communicating
- co-ordinating
- controlling *- has to be cumerical to keep control - demotivating.*
- motivating as individuals get 'lost in the crowd'. *- indiv's feel no worth.*

Expansion or merger recry.

Synergy: the idea that when two companies join together, the overall performance will be better than the sum of the two firms individually; often, expressed as 2+2=5. Can occur because of, e.g. shared research and development or shared distribution.

Overtrading: firms expand without sufficient finance; overreliant on working capital; can lead to liquidity problems (and even liquidation). Often occurs with small firms expanding too quickly.

Demerger:
In the 1990s many firms have demerged or 'unbundled' e.g. Hanson, ICI, British Gas. Reasons include:

- to raise cash
- reduce costs
- focus efforts on the 'core' business *- strip periphery business which may decrease efficiency of whole business*

working capital = current assets - current liabilities.

working capital ratio = liquidity ratio ⇒ current assets / current liabilities

The business environment

Organisations are continually reacting to changes in the environments in which they operate. To make effective decisions organisations must constantly scan their environment to identify change and prepare for it.

- **Macroenvironment:** factors beyond the immediate control of the firm

[PEST factors, Political, Economic, Social, Technological; can also be categorised as SLEEPT: social, legal, economic, environmental, political, and technological factors

- **Microenvironment:** factors in the immediate environment of the firm,

e.g. Suppliers, Workforce, Investors, Customers, Distributors. Organisations can influence micro factors more easily than macro factors.

- **Internal environment:** the functions of the organisation e.g. marketing, production, finance, and human resource management – *etcetera*

Stakeholders: stakeholders are groups with a 'stake' or interest in the organisation, e.g customers, employees, the government, shareholders. Organisations increasingly believe that success comes through co-operating with stakeholder groups.

Conflicting interests: e.g. employees may want more pay but in the short term this may have to come out of shareholders' rewards; government may want firms to hold their prices and not contribute to inflation, but owners may want a price increase to cover higher costs.

Markets: A firm's behaviour will be influenced by the type of market it operates in.

- Monopoly - in theory a single producer; in reality it occurs when one firm dominates a market; the Monopolies and Mergers Commission define a monopoly as a firm which has more than 25% of the market.

- Oligopoly - several firms dominate the market, e.g petrol, cigarettes, and washing powders. Cartel - firms acting together (colluding) to control price and output, e.g OPEC (Oil Petroleum and Exporting Countries).

- Perfect competition - many firms producing *has much the same Concentration ratio* measures the extent to which a market is controlled by a given number of firms. Usually measures their percentage of total market sales, e.g a 4 firm concentration ratio of 80% means that the largest four firms have 80% of the markets' sales.

Economic

Consumers

Distributors

Social/Cultural

Competitors

Finance | Human resources

Production | Marketing

MICROENVIRONMENT

Local community

MACRO-ENVIRONMENT

Political/Legal

Investors
Suppliers
Workforce

Technological

administration –

Human Resource Management concerned with, e.g. identifying human resource requirements, the recruitment and selection of employees, training, developing, assessing, promoting and transferring people

These functions are interrelated. For example, an increase in sales may require more employees (human resource management), more production, modifications to products (production function), or a new advertising campaign (marketing) and funds for initial promotional expenditure (finance)

Functions

Marketing: concerned with, e.g. identifying market opportunities, developing new products, distributing them, promoting and selling them.

Production: concerned with, e.g. research and development, production methods, stock control, quality control, and production levels.

Finance: concerned with, e.g. raising finance, measuring and controlling financial inflows and outflows, maintaining financial records, financial planning.

Marketing

Marketing: identifying, anticipating and meeting customer needs and wants in a mutually beneficial process. It must be beneficial for both sides; it involves meeting the organisation's objectives as well as the customers'.

organisations objectives ⇒ sales, profits, market share increase, consumers want quality & at a good price (trends)

Market and product orientation

Market orientation: The organisation focuses on customer needs and wants. The starting point of its planning is what customers want.

CUSTOMER ⟶ ORGANISATION

The purpose of a business is to get and keep a customer'.
Theodore Levitt

~ *loyalty*

Product orientation: The organisation focuses on what it wants to do and hopes customers will buy.

ORGANISATION ⟶ CUSTOMER

Product orientation can be successful if there is limited competition (e.g. a monopoly or protected market), but nowadays firms generally need to be more market oriented. For example, in the 1980s British Airways paid too much attention to their planes, and not enough to their customers; they were too product oriented.

Market myopia: marketing short sightedness; organisations which fail to appreciate changes in their markets. In the 1970s US car companies kept producing large cars despite a major increase in the price of petrol. As a result they lost market share to Japanese producers because consumers wanted smaller, fuel efficient cars.

Why is market orientation becoming more important?
Greater competition, shorter life-cycles, consumers more demanding, markets more fragmented, competitors have a clearer idea of customer needs, customers are more informed and choice is easier, markets are more open.

Asset led marketing: marketing based on the strengths of the firm rather than simply what the customer wants. The planning starts with examining the firm's assets (e.g. its staff, its location or its distribution network) as well as customer wants.

Not a good way, the customers actually want [?] effective advertising/promotion.

make a loss

More competition ∴ must respect what consumers want.

Shorter life cycles due to increase technological advance

businesses have had to adapt to what customers want, because they have no money with so much competition no ∴ can afford to ignore what consumers want.

Marketing mix: the tools of marketing.

The best known elements of the marketing mix are the four P's:

Price — what does it cost the consumer? Are there easy payment terms? Are there discounts? *what comp doing -- so it you price is product is to expensive or a copy/packaging*

Product — What does it do? What does it look like?

Promotion — How does the consumer find out about it? What are they told ? ~ *image*

Distribution (Place) — How does it get to the consumer? Direct from the manufacturer or via intermediaries? *where or self*

However, it is possible to include others: **6 p's incl...**

People — What are the staff like? Are they well trained? Cooperative? *Good with people - cs respects product*

Process — Is the buying process easy, e.g. can customers pay by credit card? How many forms are there to fill in ? Can the goods be bought by phone? Are *they moving with times ~ internet buying/catalogues*

Marketing mix - *All equally as important, if the fails then the product ex are unlikely to fail - becone all money e[?] to respectability could be lost must get it right first time through acceptance[?] e1 qualitative market research Bench & field work.*

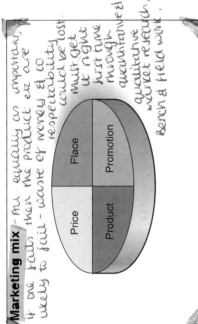

(Marketing mix diagram: Price, Product, Place, Promotion)

An example of market shares
PC sales
By volume 1995

(Pie chart)
- Apple 6%
- Toshiba 5%
- AST 5%
- Others 54%
- Dell 7%
- IBM 8%
- Compaq 15%

Niche market - a small part of the market which major producers are not concerned with, e.g Privilege offers car insurance for high risk categories such as high performance cars and young drivers. *18 [?]*

Mass market - market with a large volume or value of sales, e.g. soap powders.

Dangers of niche marketing:
- large producers may enter the market if it proves successful
- the firm may be too reliant on one product so high risk
- the firm will not benefit from economies of scale
- *swings in customer spread ~ but equally can benefit as well as lose out*

Markets

Market size - value of sales in the market; measured by number of units sold or value of sales.

Market share - a firm or product's market share is its percentage of all the sales in the market. It can be measured as a percentage of the number of units sold or of the value of sales, e.g. if market sales are £50,000 and a firm's sales are £10,000 then the firm has a 20% market share.

Marketing planning

Marketing planning sets marketing objectives; undertakes an audit of the firm's present position; and develops and implements plans to achieve its objectives, i.e. it considers: Where is the firm now? Where does it want to be? How can it get there? and then, Has it got there?

When undertaking the marketing process a firm will:

Handwritten left margin: Process must occur over & over again esp. Review, as trends change all the time & must be forecasted for.

Set corporate objectives	e.g. profitability, growth
Gather information	using market research
Assess existing situation	This is known as undertaking a MARKETING AUDIT.
	Using, e.g. product portfolio, analysis, product life cycle, and market segmentation firms produce a SWOT analysis (strengths, weaknesses, opportunities, and threats)
Set marketing objectives	e.g. market share, revenue,
Select strategy	e.g. using Ansoff matrix
Implement	using marketing mix
Review	using marketing research

Handwritten left margin: narrower, more specific though for corporation.

Budget

Handwritten left margin: like all depts.

A marketing budget will be set to control and monitor expenditure in this area.

The marketing budget may depend on

- present resources - How much do we have?
- objectives - How much do we need?
- sources of finance - How much can we raise?
- competitors - What are they spending?

Handwritten: View of marketing in co. if key dept. then may get more & past success rate of dept.

Typically firms set the budget as a percentage of this year's projected sales, as a percentage of last year's sales, or to try to match competitors' budgets.

If sales are declining, a firm might reduce its budget due to lack of finance, even though this may be the time to increase the budget to boost sales.

Handwritten: Planning in response to what the market requires.

The value of marketing planning:
- it ensures continual evaluation of objectives and strategies *— trends/fashions.*
- it should ensure efficient use of resources *— plan where money needed + contingency*
- it helps establish criteria for success; this can motivate and make it easier to monitor progress *'a set objective.*
- it improves decision making *— know what aiming for, so concentrate in area needed.*
- it involves people in discussion and should increase their commitment *— everyone has a responsibility.*
- it involves a process of analysis; this should ensure the organisation is better prepared for change.

Marketing research

Marketing research - Gathering, recording, analysing, and presenting information relevant to the marketing process. Part of marketing planning.

Market Research= constantly reviewing & asking questions in the hope consumers will give them answers.

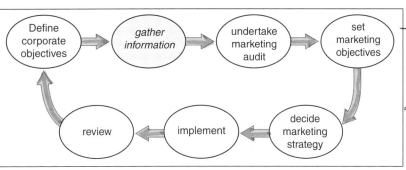

— CORPORATE OBJECTIVES.

Type of market research = important, want honesty (house to house) - People more likely to be honest on their terms - @ their house. Leaflets have poor return. Av. return ⇒ 2% so must have

Used to:

- identify opportunities and threats, e.g. How is the market changing? *could be SWOT (strengths & weaknesses)*

- analyse alternative courses of action, e.g. Would a price change be more effective than more advertising?

- review progress, e.g. monitor sales after a promotional campaign - *loyalty/opportunity buys - will they buy again, was promotion good does it say price before was too high/that people will buy with an eye to a bargain.*

When undertaking research a firm will:

- identify a problem

- decide a method of gathering data, e.g. field or desk research; postal survey or face to face

- gather the data

- analyse the data

- present its findings   PROCESSES UNDERTAKEN.

Research may be

FIELD

Primary

- first hand
- more expensive
- more likely to meet precise needs of organisation – *Find out stuff relevant.*
- gathered by field research

• *Time consuming*

DESK.

Secondary

- uses data which already exists
- cheaper
- may be in wrong format or out of date
- might be available to competitors
- gathered by desk research

For some research primary information is needed, e.g measuring customer response to a new advert.

For other research secondary information is available e.g population trends

Qualitative research: is research into peoples' motivation, feelings, behaviour. It may be undertaken in discussion groups or individual interviews

— quality information — can really help in establishing consumer views.

Sources of secondary data:

- Internal data - e.g. sales records, production records

- Government: e.g. Social Trends, Census, Annual Abstract of Statistics, Monthly Digest of Statistics (data on, e.g. output and balance of payments), Bank of England Quarterly Bulletin, Blue Book (national income)

- Independent Forecasting Groups e.g. Henley Centre

- Newspapers e.g. Financial Times

- Trade associations and trade magazines e.g. Campaign (for the advertising industry)

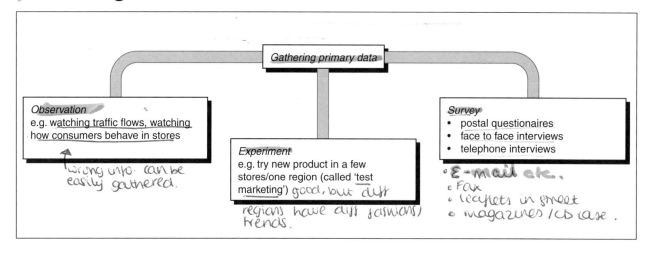

Gathering primary data

Observation
e.g. watching traffic flows, watching how consumers behave in stores

wrong info. can be easily gathered.

Experiment
e.g. try new product in a few stores/one region (called 'test marketing') *good, but diff regions have diff fashions/ trends.*

Survey
• postal questionaires
• face to face interviews
• telephone interviews

• E-mail etc.
• Fax
• leaflets in street
• magazines / cd case.

Internal v external data

Internal data is information gathered within the firm itself, e.g. from its own sales records. *ie Marks & Tesco (loyalty cards → coupons (extra sales))*

External data is information gathered from outside of the firm, e.g. from customers, from competitors, from market research agencies.

Samples:

Population: the total number of items or people the researcher is interested in.

only done every 10 years by gov.

Census - a survey of the total population. Not usually feasible due to time and expense. *→ can only do a % of or target market of.*

To save time and money, researchers may take a sample. This is a small group which is thought to represent the market as a whole. Sampling is subject to error because the sample may not be representative. Using statistical techniques, the results are expressed in terms of probability and the confidence with which they can be used. For example, when estimating future sales, researchers may produce a 95% confidence interval of £120m to £130m. This means that 95% of the time sales will be between these two values; the firm can be 95% confident that sales will be between £120 and £130m.

Market researchers are only truely happy when confidence level = 95%+ or 19/20. it means that the product is practically a sure thing - though you never know in respect to trends/fashions.

Types of sample:

random number chart.

Random - every member of the population has an equal chance of selection *- paid by gov.*

Stratified - the sample is divided into segments (strata) e.g. male/female and a random sample is selected from each segment in given proportions, e.g. 3 men to every 7 women.

ie if 1/4 of men buy Product A & rest = 3/4 of women. Then those asked will be 1 man to every 3 women.

Cluster - the 'population' is separated into different clusters, usually geographical areas; samples- are taken in each area. *ie sun product tested on those living in coastal regions.*

Systematic - every 'n'th item of the population selected, e.g. every fiftieth person on an electoral register is chosen

respondants drawn from sub-group ie women 35 - 55 yrs for anti wrinkle cream.

Quota - a researcher is given specific characteristics, e.g. forty people over 30 and then finds people who meet this criteria. This is a non-random sample, e.g. if the researcher stands on a street corner, he or she can only ask people who happen to be passing. Other people have no chance of being asked.

if standing on street corner → need to count people to be impartial.

Evaluating research

How much will it cost? How long will it take? What alternatives are there? how important is it that we know? What is the risk if we do not do research? How reliable will the findings be? (i.e. if the research was repeated would the firm get the same results?)

Research does not guarantee success but can help to reduce the risk.

Not all research uses formal researching methods. Some decisions are based on intuition or hunch.

if research takes a long time to collect then by time all is collected, it could be incorrect esp if product relies on fashion trends, otherwise competitors may already have launched.

Segmentation

Segmentation: identifying groups of relatively similar needs and wants within a market. The firm can then develop an appropriate marketing mix for each segment. The aim is to meet customer needs more precisely. The problem is that it may cost more to develop new versions of a product or service.

but co. would be looked on favourably for reaching consumers as relative individuals with diff. needs & wants

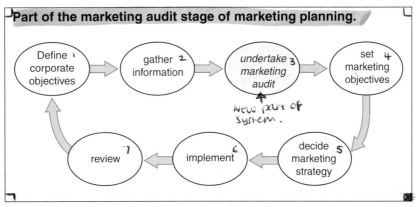

Part of the marketing audit stage of marketing planning.

Define ₁ corporate objectives → gather ₂ information → undertake ₃ marketing audit → set ₄ marketing objectives

New part of system.

review ₇ ← implement ₆ ← decide ₅ marketing strategy

Makes marketing easier to narrow target market. Age = sensitive area.

Methods of segmentation:

- Age
  e.g. magazines for different age groups (e.g. Just 17), adult snacks (e.g Phileas Fogg), Landmark Express offer cheaper car insurance for people over 45, Club 18-30 holidays obviously target a particular age-group.

- Gender
  e.g. certain cars are targeted at women drivers some toys are aimed more at boys (e.g. Action Man), others target girls (e.g. Barbie).

- Socio-Economic groups
  e.g. newspapers target different Socio-Economic groups.

e.g.

A	upper middle class	higher managerial/professional e.g lawyer
B	middle class	middle managerial/administrative/professional e.g manager
C1	lower middle class	supervisors, clerks, junior managers e.g shop assistant
C2	skilled working class	skilled manual worker e.g mechanic
D	working class	semi skilled/unskillled manual e.g cleaner
E	subsistence level	unemployed or state pensioner

- Location
  e.g. board games sell better in colder climates; outdoor games are more popular in warmer regions

- An individual's stage in the life cycle
  e.g the housing market consists of first time buyers, people trading up and retirement buyers; magazines – *Practical Parenting*

- Family size
  e.g family packs of food, design of houses

- Usage rates
  e.g frequent wash shampoo / *trainers & sport equip ⇒ fashion, sport, resting clothes.*

- Lifestyle
  e.g convenient, microwaveable food for young, single, working people *→ life more hectic*

- Benefit
  e.g people buy toothpaste for different benefits, including the taste, fresh breath and to keep their teeth white, *fight decay, fluoride for kids. Smokers.*

- Psychographical (motives for buying)
  e.g. reasons why people buy chocolates include to reward themselves, to relax, to share, to give to others.

• Culture

practical usage.

Targeting

Targeting: selecting which segments to aim for. This depends on the size and expected profitability of a segment and its fit with the firm's resources and objectives.

what are other products it produces? Go for similar age group, or diff → to decrease risk.

Undifferentiated marketing: one product for the whole market, e.g. WD40 is used by a range of buyers to stop doors squeaking, protect engine parts from damp, loosen rusty bolts, loosen limescale..........

Concentrated marketing: a particular segment is targeted, e.g. 18-30 holidays

Differentiated marketing: a separate mix is developed for each segment, e.g. full fat milk, semi skimmed, skimmed, breakfast milk, goat's milk

Product portfolio analysis

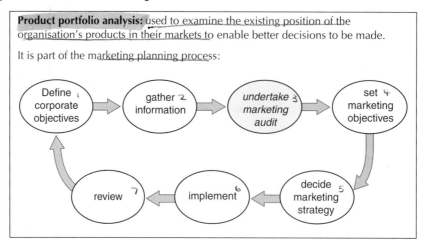

Product portfolio analysis: used to examine the existing position of the organisation's products in their markets to enable better decisions to be made.

It is part of the marketing planning process:

Boston Box Model: BOSTON MATRIX

One of the most well known methods of product portfolio analysis is the Boston Box. It shows what percentage of the market each product has (from high to low) and the rate at which the market as a whole is growing (from high to low).

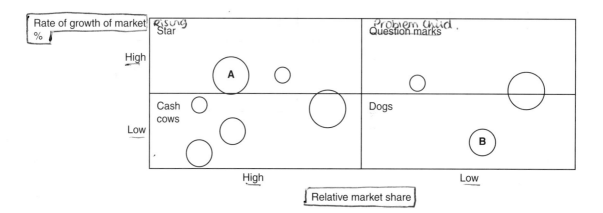

Each circle in the above diagram represents a particular product produced by the firm. The area of the circle represents the value of its sales, e.g. product A sells more than product B

RISING

Stars: high share of fast growing market e.g. vodaphone mobile phones May require considerable amounts of cash to keep competitive competition	**Question marks, problem children, oil rigs:** small share of fast growing markets; potentially successful but need protection and investment. May become stars but may be pushed out. - Need to be nurtured.
Cash cows: large share of slow growing market such as a market which has matured, e.g. Marmite, Oxo cubes, Heinz Ketchup. These products have already been developed, and promoted, and generate relatively high levels of cash. This can be used to develop and protect other products.	**Dogs:** small share of slow growing market Could be revived (e.g. Lucozade) but may be dropped. Dogs often take up more management time than they are worth.

A business does not want too many of any ↑∴
Problem child ⇒ potentially
Rising stars, & Rising stars
potential cash cows. Must
not just think of terms
at present, but also for the
FUTURE (of product & co.)

Options for decision makers include:

Hold - attempt to maintain existing market position, e.g. with strong cash cows — for present

Build - invest to develop position, e.g. with problemchild question marks. May involve sacrificing short term profits. - For future.

Harvest - aim for short term profits, do not invest long term, e.g. possible with cash cows — Present - what will they do for future.

Divest - get rid of product, e.g. with dogs — only if can't be uplifted. Lucozade was revived.

Depends on what was position - was it any of other 3 before dog.

Product life cycle — *less sophisticated than the Boston matrix.*

Product life cycle: shows stages in a product's life. It is a model used to aid decision making. It is part of the marketing planning process:

```
Define 1 corporate objectives → gather 2 information → undertake 3 marketing audit → set marketing objectives → decide 5 marketing strategy → 4 implement → review → (back to Define corporate objectives)
```

The shape and length of the life cycle will differ from one product to another. Some life cycles last years (e.g. Kellogg's Cornflakes); others are more short-lived (e.g. Teenage Mutant Ninja Turtles.)

Stages of the life cycle: development, introduction, growth, maturity, decline

	D Develop-ment	I Intro-duction	G Growth	M Maturity	S Decline	A
		electric cars	CD ROMs	colour tv's	black & white tv's	
		video 'phones	fax machines	washing machines	typewriters	

(market saturation)

Development — Product is being developed and tested. This may take years, e.g. a new car or new film or may take hours, e.g. a new recipe in a restaurant. Losses are often made due to heavy development costs.

scientific research may take years/ essential to have other products in Boston matrix.

(making place → Boston matrix)

Introduction — Sales often slow. Distributors may be reluctant to make a new unproved product. Heavy promotion to make consumers aware. High level of risk. High unit production costs – no economies of scale.

once product successful advert. scale.

→*Growth* — Sales begin to grow rapidly. Competition beginning to enter the market. Profits usually made.

Maturity — Cost per unit falling - economies of scale. More competition. Promotion stresses differences with competition. The firm will try to develop/maintain brand loyalty.

depending on product, co. view an its success, trends et fashion, a co. will have to decide whether it will extend the life cycle or let it die a natural death.

Decline — Sales declining. Profits falling. Substitutes appear.

Many ideas, but at advanced stage if more et more products fall out.

Many products don't pass this stage.

Marketing 25

Millions

Life cycles of LPs, cassettes, CDs and singles

(Graph axis values: 120, 90, 60, 30, 0; years 1973, 1978, 1983, 1988, 1994; labelled Singles, LPs, CDs, Cassettes; axis "Sales")

(Sales vs Time graph with extension strategies)

Extension strategies: attempts to prolong the maturity stage and not let sales decline. A firm may:

- Modify the product, e.g. 'new' 'added' 'extra' ingredients – *often do with shampoo – Organics.*
- Promote more heavily, e.g. more advertising */2 for the price of 1.*
- Develop complimentary products, e.g. extend the product range - add shaving cream and after shave to shampoo and conditioner products – *mars → icecream, mars, mars king etc. walnut, blue star.*
- Find new uses for the product – *sports equipment – lycra, sportsleisurewear. Growing gym – trim breath a prevent room decay after yearseng*
- Attempt to increase usage, e.g. encourage customers to eat cereals in the evenings as well as the mornings *& sports equip ↑*

FAD

A 'fad' product, e.g. Rubik's cube

NEW USES

New uses found for product, e.g. 'Kevlar' material used for bullet proof vests, skis, boats, helmets

REVIVED

Product is revived. e.g. Lucozade, Flared trousers, Ovaltine

Product life cycle continued

SWOT analysis:

Process of analysing the strengths, weaknesses, opportunities, and threats facing an organisation. Aim: to improve decision making and develop an appropriate marketing strategy. Part of the marketing process.

Define corporate objectives → gather information → undertake Marketing audit → set marketing objectives → decide marketing strategy → implement → review.

Strengths: e.g strong brand name, good sales team, skilled employees, good industrial relations
↑ *motivated workforce .
high % of market share.*

Weaknesses: e.g limited availability of finance, poor distribution network, limited production capacity. *ageing workforce without new blood.*
Strengths and weaknesses relate to the internal and existing position of an organisation.

Opportunities: e.g new markets, new products and processes

Threats: e.g changing social trends, new legislation, technological change, *competition.*

Opportunities and threats relate to external future changes.

Value of life cycle:

highlights different stages in a typical life cycle and the need to adjust marketing strategies and tactics at each stage. However, it is only a model. The decision maker must take account of different markets and different ways in which products may develop. There is a danger of it become self fulfiling, e.g because firms expect a decline in sales they fail to devote enough resources to a product to enable sales to be maintained.

and good producers are lost .

Positioning:

How a product is perceived by a consumer relative to its competitors.
e.g. stronger, faster

Positioning map: illustrates the position of products relative to each other,

e.g one consumer's perception of the chocolate market may be:

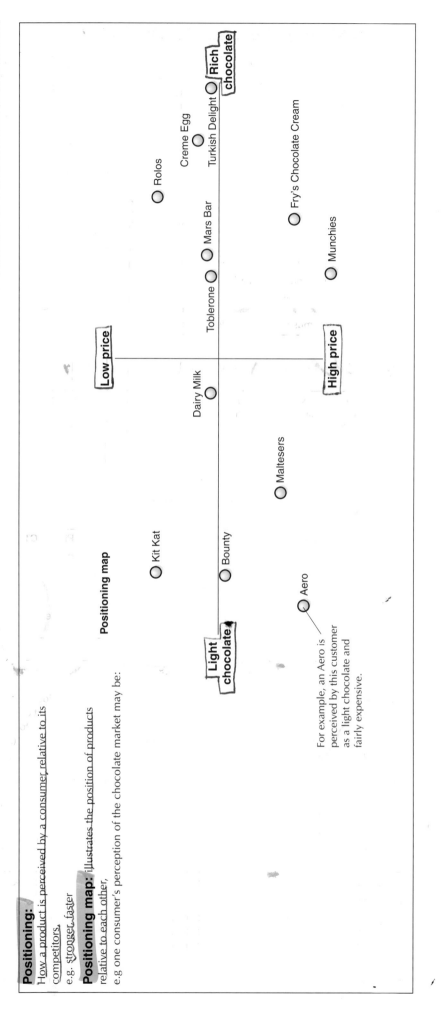

Positioning map

For example, an Aero is perceived by this customer as a light chocolate and fairly expensive.

Setting marketing objectives

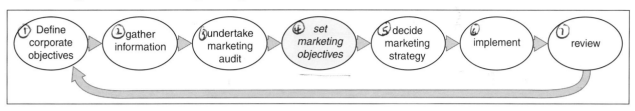

Marketing objectives are derived from financial objectives, e.g.

- a rate of return of 12% over the next five years
- net profits of £2.5m this year
- produce a cashflow of £3m this year

Marketing objectives, e.g :

- increase sales volume by 5% this year
- increase revenue by 12% this year
- increase customer awareness by 8% this year

These objectives must be quantifiable and have a time limit.

Selecting a marketing strategy

Once the existing position of an organisation's products has been analysed and the firm has undertaken a SWOT analysis, it can select an appropriate marketing strategy.

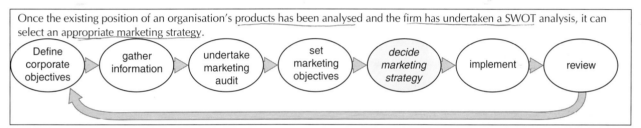

Marketing strategies can be examined using the Ansoff Matrix

		PRODUCT	
		Existing	New
MARKET	Existing	Market Penetration _change price / promotion_	New Product Development
	New	Market Development _overseas / new segment_	Diversification _new market with new prod._

Market penetration: attempt to gain a greater share of an existing market, e.g. by changing price or increasing promotion. Involves changing elements of the marketing mix such as the price and promotion to increase sales.

New product development: _develop new product for existing market_

Stages

1. Idea generation - generate ideas 'internally' (e.g. from employees or research and development department) or 'externally' (e.g. from patent office, external inventors, universities, competitors, consumers) _via market research_
2. Analyse - assess feasibility (also called 'screening')
3. Development - produce mock ups or prototypes
4. Product Testing - test for safety and quality
5. Test marketing - test sales in selected outlets / _regions_
6. Launch - sell nationally or 'roll out' (gradually introducing in one region then another)

Market development: launching existing product into new markets, e.g. sell overseas or target new segment.

- Entering overseas markets. Consider for example the political stability, legal differences, economic factors, social and cultural factors. Methods of entering overseas markets: export, use agent, franchise or license, joint venture, direct investment.
- Moving into new segment, e.g. Dr Martens moved from workwear to fashion wear

Diversification: enter new market with new product. A high risk element due to unfamiliarity; but spreads risk - less vulnerable to changes in one market, e.g. Michelin tyres, maps and guidebooks.

Price

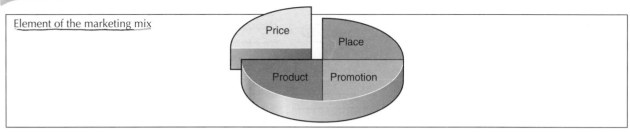

Element of the marketing mix

Price · Place · Product · Promotion

The price of a good or service may depend on:

high or low order good

1. • **costs** - organisations will generally want to cover their costs to make a profit for investment and to reward their owners — *dividends. Pay staff.*

2. • **demand and elasticity** - i.e. What is the level of demand and how sensitive is demand to price?

3. • **competition** - i.e How similar are their products? What price are they charging?

4. • **government** - e.g. the Government places indirect taxes (such as VAT) on most goods, which increases costs

5. • **objectives** - e.g. short term or long term profits

quantafiable & with time constraint.

• **stage of the life cycle** e.g. the price is more likely to increase in the growth phase and fall in decline

• rest of the mix, e.g. Is it positioned as a more exclusive item than competitors, products? → *where how what.*

The price is likely to be higher when:

• the good is heavily branded — ∴ *loyalty / fashion*

• the good is distributed to exclusive outlets

• it is a speciality good *.. to cover R&D costs mainly*

• the good is at the growth stage of the life cycle

• the firm is following a skimming strategy

Methods of pricing include:

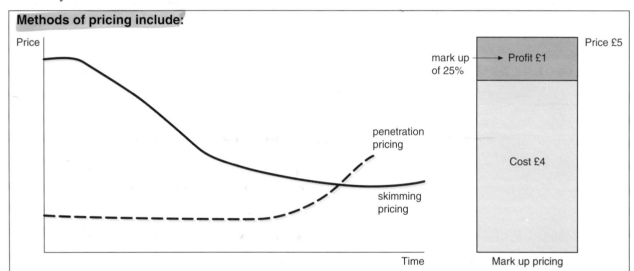

penetration pricing

skimming pricing

Price | Time

mark up of 25% → Profit £1

Cost £4

Price £5

Mark up pricing

Skimming - high initial price to cover initial research and development costs quickly. Suitable for an innovative or protected product (e.g. a patent) and where demand is price inelastic

Penetration - low price to gain market share quickly. Suitable when there are substantial economies of scale or when demand is price sensitive

Competitor based - suitable when the market is competitive and price comparisons are easy, e.g. shopping goods

esp if price determined from market research, on street, people will not be truly honest in fear of looking 'miserly'

Demand based or perceived value - firm tries to estimate what people are willing to pay. This is the most market oriented approach, but it can be difficult to discover what people are willing to pay.

Cost based pricing - the firm adds an amount on to costs to decide on the price, i.e it adds a mark up on to the costs. This is a simple and, therefore, popular pricing method, but ignores demand conditions (see diagram).

Cost per unity + % mark up.

Predatory pricing - a firm undercuts competitors to remove competition; once competitors leave, the price is increased again. This policy can lead to a price war in which all firms try to undercut each other. *? bad for co's good for customers.*

Price discrimination - charging different prices for the same product/service, e.g. some taxis charge different prices late at night, rail fares are often higher at peak times; and some bars have 'happy hours' when drinks are cheaper. The firm will increase the price in segments where demand is price inelastic and decrease the price when demand is price elastic. *Or where product = same, sold in diff places ∴ fashion victims pay more than others.*

Loss leader - product sold below cost to generate orders for other product e.g. retailers put well known brand in shop windows and sell at a loss to attract people into the store.

Psychological pricing - focuses on consumer's perception of price, e.g. charging high prices to convey quality charging £2.99 rather than £3.00 because people regard it as 'over £2' rather than in the £3 band, and stressing a reduction in price (e.g. was £20, now £12).

what the customer will bare (skimming)
follow the leader (follow competition)

Product

Element of the marketing mix

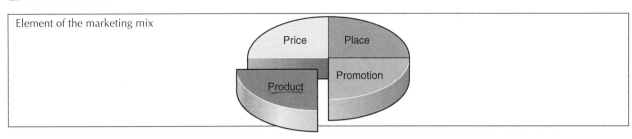

A product can be examined on three levels:

Core: the benefits of the product, e.g. microwave = convenience, after shave = attraction

Tangible: the actual features of the product, e.g. what it looks like, what it weighs, what it does, how it is packaged

Augmented: other services or benefits that are obtained, e.g. delivery, guarantees, servicing.

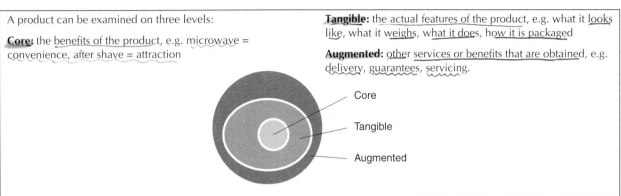

The quality of a product depends on its:

1. • performance - e.g the speed of a car, the power of a microwave

2. • features - the extras, e.g air conditioning or sunroof on a car

3. • ease of servicing - How easy is it to fix?

4. • reliability - How likely is it to go wrong in, say, the first year?

5. • durability - How long will it last?

6. • aesthetics - What does it look like?

7. • economics - What does it cost to produce? Can it be sold at a profit?

8. • brand name — *if brand name then quality (high) is expected more than cheaper varieties.*

9. • ease of manufacture

making 2 brands similar - people could mistake one from other if in hurry.

Product differentiation: anything which distinguishes the product from another in the eyes of the consumer

Product cannibalisation: when the sales of one product which a firm has launched reduce the sales of another of its existing products.

one takes over other (engulfs it)

Product continued

Types of product
Consumer goods:

layer order goods usually →

Convenience items
Consumer searches for nearest shop and does not take long thinking about the purchase decision.
Extensive distribution.

Types include:

staple items - regularly bought, e.g. milk, newspaper

emergency items, e.g. plasters

impulse items: chewing gum - consumer did not go in to buy; afterthought

Shopping goods
Consumer shops around, e.g. for tv, washing machine
Often distributed in city centres

Consumers take time to buy; think about it; compare goods and prices; look for the best value

Speciality goods
unique/'special' goods; consumers willing to make special effort to buy, e.g. Porsche, Armani suits.

Exclusive distribution.

special furniture

Consumer durables
bought by households but not consumed immediately *TV's washing machines*

Non Durables
Bought by households and consumed immediately *food.*

Industrial goods - price & aftersale service = essential. Though will spend longer on chosing higher order goods

Industrial goods:
Raw Materials - e.g. oranges, oil. Prices may fluctuate with supply and demand; often traded on world-wide markets. Little distinction between products; limited branding.

Manufactured parts - usually sold directly to manufacturer; price and service very important; branding and advertising less important.

Supplies - e.g light bulbs, soap. Little time spent in purchase; bought from intermediaries; price important; little brand preference.

Installations - capital goods, e.g. factories or new production equipment; long purchasing process; personal selling is important; often a long negotiation period; the technical aspects of the product are vital; price inelastic. Bought direct from manufacturer. Sellers have to be willing to design to order.

Accessory equipment - e.g desks. Often bought from wholesalers; competitive market; buyers likely to 'shop around'. many buyers; small orders.

---

build up correspondance, & negioation occurs because sales = on larger scale & need to be close oo often sales will be every year or so.
Also products are and more complex oo need close talks - to explain products.

	Industrial goods	Consumer goods
Number of customers	Relatively few, *for a co.* professional buyers	Many - *individuals.*
Relations with customers	Close	Often distant
Promotion	Often personal selling	Advertising more important
Distribution	Direct; few if any intermediaries	More intermediaries

---

Copyright: creator's or legal owner's rights in creative works such as paintings, writings, photographs or TV commercials. Copyright occurs automatically and does not need registering.

Trademark: a symbol used by a producer to identify a product which is legally protected under Trade Marks Act 1938. Trade Marks (amendment) Act 1984 - trademarks registered with Patent Office.

Patent: a licence which prevents the copying of an idea; aims to protect inventors of a new product or process. New inventions protected for 15 years. Must be registered with Patent Office. This protection encourages research, allows inventors monopoly profits to reward their ideas, and encourages more products to be developed.

The American Can Co.'s patent for the ring-pull has earned them over £50m.

Logo: visual symbol of a product or organisation e.g. Shell's 'shell'; Apple's 'apple', MGM's lion.

Distribution *Place .*

The channel of distribution describes how the title of ownership passes from the manufacturer to the consumer.

Element of the marketing mix.

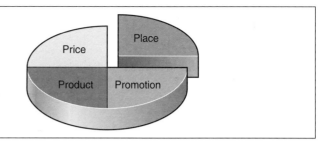

Levels of distibution

0 level

Manufacturer ➔ Consumer
e.g. services, mail order

1 level

Manufacturer ➔ Retailer ➔ Consumer
e.g. many shopping goods *- goods like TV's.*

2 level

Manufacturer ➔ Wholesaler ➔ Retailer ➔ Consumer
e.g. many convenience goods *- newspapers -*

Changing nature of distribution: major retailers such as Sainsbury's have become much more important, becoming 'channel captains', i.e. they dominate the channel compared to manufacturers. They have also reduced the role of wholesalers and increased one level rather than two level channels.

wholesalers gets proportion ↑ profits, ∴ less productive

Intermediaries: Intermediaries reduce the number of transactions between retailers and producers:

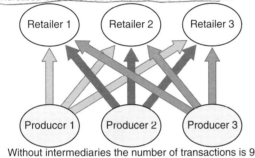

Retailer 1   Retailer 2   Retailer 3

Producer 1   Producer 2   Producer 3

Without intermediaries the number of transactions is 9

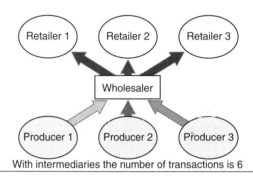

Retailer 1   Retailer 2   Retailer 3

Wholesaler

Producer 1   Producer 2   Producer 3

With intermediaries the number of transactions is 6

they manage to achieve economies of scale →

Intermediaries

Wholesalers: 'break bulk' i.e. buy in large quantities from manufacturers and break into smaller quantities for retailers.

Agents: do not take ownership of the goods. They represent a firm and try to gain sales for it. Receive a commission. Often used to enter overseas markets.

In consumer goods.

Types of channel

Exclusive
Very limited number of outlets; suitable for speciality goods

Selective
Selected outlets with suitable environments & image; suitable for shopping goods

Extensive
Widespread distribution; suitable for e.g. convenience goods

Choosing a channel:
- Costs
- Alternatives - when Avon could not distribute cosmetics through department stores it sold door to door.
- Type of product - industrial products tend to have shorter channels as they have fewer customers and a more complex product which needs detailed explanation. Fragile products are also likely to have a direct channel. Basic low value items with many consumers widely spread geographically are likely to have long channels with many intermediaries. *- Newspapers*

Distribution strategies

Push strategy: manufacturer forces goods through channels by giving intermediaries incentives, e.g. discounts, higher margins, display items.

manufacturer ⟶ intermediaries

Pull strategy: focus is on consumers, by appealing to consumers directly. The aim is to make them demand the product and force intermediaries to stock the goods.

manufacturer ⟵ intermediaries

force goods on intermediaries via incentives

get consumers to demand product ∴

Promotion

Promotion involves communication about the product or service.

Element of the marketing mix.

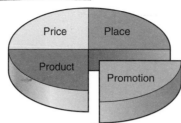

Objectives may be:
- to make consumers aware of, e.g. new product launch
- To get loyalty /more frequent buys / bigger market share (profits)
- to remind consumers
- to persuade consumers

Methods of promoting:

(2 for 1)

- **Sale promotion:** short term incentives to increase sales, e.g. coupons, competitions. Effect is often to destroy loyalty to other brands and encourage brand switching; when promotion ends consumers often switch to another brand's offer. Sales promotion is called below the line promotional activity.

  TV radio magazine newspapers

- **Advertising:** paid for communication. It is called an 'above the line' promotional activity.

- **Public relations:** involves managing relations with different publics, e.g. the media, consumers, pressure groups, investors. May involve getting media coverage of event or product launch or generally creating a favourable impression and generating word of mouth interest. The difficulty is that it is not easy to control what others write or say.

- **Personal selling:** use of sales representatives.

- **Direct mailing:** information is sent through the post
- **Exhibitions and trade fairs**
- **Merchandising:** an attempt to influence consumers at point of sale, e.g. display material
- **Packaging:** e.g. design, shape, information displayed on it
- **Branding:** name or design which identifies the products or services of a manufacturer and distinguishes them from competitors.

Tesco

Brands

Own label (own brand) - retailers use own name (e.g. Sainsbury's), rather than a manufacturer's.

Family brand - business name on a number of products, e.g. Heinz beans, soup, spaghetti

Individual product branding, i.e. each product has a different brand name, e.g. Van den Bergh produces Flora, Delight, Krona, Stork, Blue Brand and Echo margarines.

Brand leader - brand with the highest market share

AIDA

Advertising should seek to :

A attract _attention_   **I** create _interest_
D develop a _desire_   **A** lead to _action_ (purchase)

(the **AIDA** model)

Advertising occurs on posters, in newspapers, in magazines, on television, and on the radio.

When deciding on the appropriate medium, advertisers should consider: the cost, the target audience, and the appropriateness of the chosen medium.

Controls on advertising:

1. Advertising Standards Authority is a voluntary body which seeks to ensure adverts are 'legal decent honest, truthful and do not cause widespread offence'. _Benetton (offensive)_

2. Independent Television Commission - controls advertising on tv and radio.

Corporate advertising: promoting the company as a whole rather than a particular product

Using the promotional mix

Industrial goods are generally sold to a few professional buyers. Advertising is less important apart from, e.g. the trade press, whereas personal selling is vital. SUMMARY

With consumer goods, such as jeans, advertising to the final consumer is more common. Personal selling is important to get the items distributed but advertising pulls the consumers into the shops.

Arguments for advertising
- informs
- makes people aware
- creates jobs
- creative/art form

Arguments against
- adds 'unnecessary' costs
- persuades people to buy goods/services they do not really want
- time consuming
- encourages the 'wrong' kind of values and behaviour, e.g. greed

Elasticity of demand

Elasticity of demand measures the responsiveness of demand to a change in a variable such as price, income or advertising. It measures how much demand changes (in %) compared to the variable.

Sweets   *Armani suit / levi's etc.*

Elastic and inelastic

If demand changes more than the variable (in %), it is sensitive or elastic.

e.g. if demand increases 30% following a 10% price cut, the price elasticity of demand is 3. It is elastic because demand has changed three times price.

If demand changes less than the variable, it is insensitive or inelastic.

e.g. if demand changes 5% following a 10% price cut, the price elasticity of demand is 0.5. It is inelastic because demand changes half as much as the change in price.

% change in demand	:	% change in variable

Elastic:– *over 1*
% change in demand is greater than % change in variable

% change in demand	:	% change in variable

Inelastic:– *under 1.*
% change in demand is less than % change in variable

Price elasticity: sensitivity of demand to changes in price

Measured by the percentage change in demand compared to the percentage change in price:

$$\text{Price elasticity} = \frac{\%\ \text{change in demand}}{\%\ \text{change in price}}$$

%Δ in D
%Δ in P

If demand is not sensitive to price (price inelastic) the firm is more likely to increase price to increase revenue, because the increase in price leads to a smaller decrease in quantity demanded (in %).

If demand is sensitive to price (price elastic) the firm will lower price to increase revenue because a lower price will lead to a larger increase in quantity demanded (in %)

Whether an increase in revenue will also increase profit depends on what happens to costs as output changes.

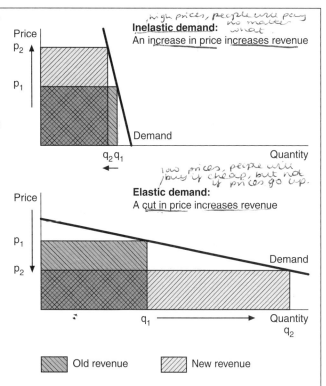

high prices, people will pay no matter what

Inelastic demand:
An increase in price increases revenue

low prices, people will buy if cheap, but not if prices go up.

Elastic demand:
A cut in price increases revenue

Old revenue	New revenue

Goods are likely to be price inelastic if:

- only a small percentage of income is spent on them, e.g. milk

- there are few substitutes, e.g. innovative products, protected by patents

- they are addictive goods, e.g. cigarettes

- they are paid for by someone else, e.g. business travel paid for by the firm

- they are heavily branded – *loyalty to do with fashion/perceived taste.*

The price elasticity will often be given as a negative number. This is because when price goes down demand usually goes up and vice versa - i.e. price and quantity move in opposite directions. This results in a negative answer. When considering the price elasticity in business studies the sign is not important and should be ignored. i.e. -4 = 4 elastic) and -0.7 = 0.7 (inelastic).

Ignore (-) minus signs in elasticity.
>1 = elastic
<1 = inelastic

(factors)
Price
Income
Advertising

income elastic = non essentials, luxuries.

income inelastic = essentials

+ = Normal good (I↑ D↑)

− = Inferior Good (I↑ D↓)

Income elasticity: shows sensitivity of demand to income

Measured by the percentage change in demand compared to the percentage change in income.

$$\text{Income elasticity} = \frac{\% \text{ change in demand}}{\% \text{ change in income}}$$

Some goods will be income elastic (i.e. sensitive to income changes) others will be inelastic.

Income elastic goods and services may include: overseas holidays, sports cars, washing machines, dishwashers, and houses

Income inelastic may include: potatoes, pencils, milk, and newspapers

Industries such as the holiday industry are, therefore, more sensitive to booms and slumps in the economy than the pencil industry.

A *positive* sign shows that when income increases, demand increases as well (or vice versa), i.e. both demand and income move together. This is true for NORMAL GOODS.

A *negative* sign occurs if demand falls when income increases (i.e. demand and income move in opposite directions); this happens with INFERIOR GOODS - as consumers get more income they switch to more luxurious options. A bicycle may be an inferior good for *some* consumers; with more income consumers switch to a car.

If this is between two products in the same firm, it is called 'Product Cannibalism'.

+ = SUBSTITUTES (A and D for
↑ in Price = ↑D for Ⓐ & ↓D for Ⓑ
for B

(−) =
COMPLEMENTS

↑ in Price ⇒ ↓D for Ⓐ & Ⓑ
of Ⓑ

Cross elasticity: shows how responsive demand for one good (A) is to changes in the price of another good (B);

$$\text{Cross elasticity} = \frac{\% \text{ change of demand for A}}{\% \text{ change in price of B.}}$$

The larger the value of the cross elasticity, the greater the relationship between the two goods, e.g. demand for The Times is likely to be more sensitive to changes in the price of The Independent compared to changes in the price of The Sun as the first two are more similar.

If the cross elasticity has a *positive* sign, the goods are SUBSTITUTES. An *increase* in the price of one good leads to an *increase* in demand for the other and consumers switch, e.g. IBM and Compaq

If the cross elasticity is *negative* the two goods are COMPLEMENTS. An *increase* in the price of one good leads to a decrease in demand for it and a *decrease* in demand for the other good, e.g. personal computers and computer disks

---

value of 3 = demand x 3 more than change in advertising expenditure elasticity (Elastic)

value 0.3 = demand changes 0.3 (inelastic)

+ = demand ↑ with advertising

−) = demand ↓ with advertising ie 'Don't drink & Drive'

Advertising elasticity: shows how responsive demand is to changes in advertising.

$$\text{Advertising elasticity} = \frac{\% \text{ change in demand}}{\% \text{ change in elasticity expenditure}}$$

The larger the value of the advertising elasticity, the greater the relationship between advertising and demand. A value of 3 means that demand changes 3 times more than the change in advertising expenditure elasticity (Elastic); a value of 0.3 means demand changes 0.3 times as much.

If the answer has a *positive* value this means that demand increases with more advertising; if it is *negative*, demand decreases with advertising (e.g a 'Don't drink and drive' campaign).

Sources of Finance

Short term finance: for day to day requirements:
Overdraft- very flexible; interest paid when the account is overdrawn and usually lower than a bank loan. However, amount owed can be demanded back at any moment.

Not good to keep on having overdrafts, bank may force you to take up a loan (higher interest rates)

Medium term finance:
- Bank loan - borrowed over a fixed period of time. Loan is repaid in regular installments. + interest.
- Hire purchase - often used to buy equipment. Usually involves a down payment and then regular instalments. *when all instalments paid off, you own the piece of equipment*
- Trade credit - buying items from suppliers and paying later, e.g. 30 days.
- Leasing - equipment is rented. This avoids a large initial outflow and equipment may be repaired and updated easily. - *co leasing from must pay for maintenence, but if using equipment regularly, prob. cheaper to buy it.*
- Debt factoring - firms borrow money using their debtors (i.e. the amount owed) as security. Debt factor lends to firm and takes over responsibility for debtors.

co. doing factoring will be given a receipt of what is owed, they will pay the owner of receipt, less a percentage (5-10%) then the debtor has to pay the co. the full receipt.
Benefits
- co. gets money (but risk)
- owner of receipt, gets most of money (bar the 5-10%) quickly- esp. useful if debtor.

Long term finance:
- Issue share capital - may involve more owners and loss of control; shares may be sold to existing shareholders (rights issue), to general public (public or direct issue), to merchant bank which then sells them to general public (offer for sale) or to private clients (placing). *Easy way to get money, though some drawbacks.* *＊given 1st opportunity.*
- Debentures - IOU certificates; the buyer is paid interest each year and receives the amount they lent back after a fixed period of time; the buyer is not an owner of the company. *A loan with good returns - can be done by individuals.*
- Mortgage - borrowings using property as collateral (security) to guarantee the loan. - *very long term, high interest rates.*
- Government assistance - e.g. grants, *tax aid in enterprise zones.*
- Venture capital - money lent to small firms (usually combination of loans and share capital) to finance new firms which are risky and may have difficulty getting finance from elsewhere.

Sources of internal finance
- Profit
- Sale of assets
- Working capital (e.g. reduce stocks)
- *redundancies*

Sources of external finance
- Sale of shares
- Loans

Debt v. equity, i.e. loans v. shares   *can upset owners, cutting divivdends.*

Debt
- Interest must be paid before owners receive dividends
- Lenders can force liquidation
- Higher risk - interest must be paid, even if profits are low

Sell shares
- Lose ownership and control with new investors
- Owners expect dividends although may be possible to delay

could be seen as weak & preditory take over bid could result

more people to give dividends to

The gearing ratio measures long term borrowing as a percentage of the firm's long term finance (capital employed); highly geared = high percentage of borrowings.

As long as gearing is below 50% then borrowing is not too high.

Accounts

Accounts: numerate information to help decision making. Accounting collects data of a firm's activities, turns this into monetary values; and presents findings in a suitable form for the decision maker.

Accounting is part of the decision making process:

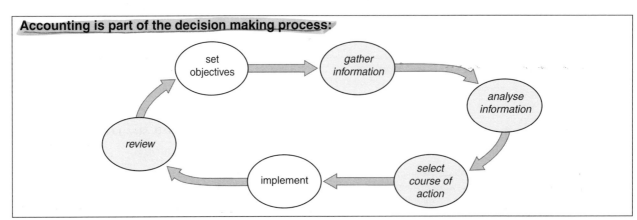

Accounting information is used by

see what kind of debtors firm is.

- outsiders   e.g. potential investors, lenders, government, suppliers   *tax.*   *see if they are good debtors. how credit worthy they are, liquidity, are they good payers.*

- insiders   e.g. managers, employees

see where they stand.

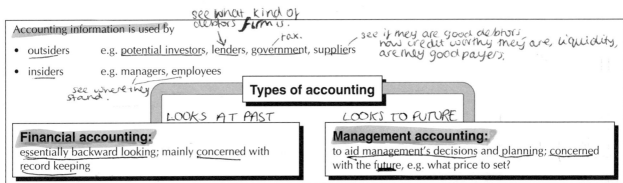

Types of accounting

LOOKS AT PAST   LOOKS TO FUTURE

Financial accounting:
essentially backward looking; mainly concerned with record keeping

Management accounting:
to aid management's decisions and planning; concerned with the future, e.g. what price to set?

Accounting principles

The getting of a good.

Realisation: a sale is realised when a good is delivered; i.e. when goods are delivered they can be recorded as revenue even if cash has not been received.

Matching: costs must be matched to the period when they are incurred, e.g. if a firm buys £300 of materials and only uses up a third in this period, the costs are £100; £200 is left in stock.

Materiality: deciding whether an item is worth treating as an asset and depreciating, e.g. if only a third of a £1.50 jar of coffee has been used by the end of the period, the cost should be entered as 50p and the remaining value of the asset recorded as £1. However, items as small are this are often 'written off', i.e. all of the £1.50 would be put as a cost in one go. This is because they are not material enough for a firm to bother measuring exactly how much has been used up.

Revenue – income
costs ⇒ outgoings

Prudence: accountants should be conservative when producing accounts; if in doubt they should underestimate revenue and overestimate costs.*

Consistency: accounting information should be consistently gathered and presented from one year to the next, e.g. a firm should not simply change its depreciation policies from one year to another just to make its results look better. *(window dressing)*

The accounting profession and the interpretation and development of accounting principles is regulated in the UK by the Accounting Standards Board (ASB).

The ASB is responsible for producing:

① *FRED* Financial Reporting Exposure Drafts - draft versions of proposed new accounting standards

② *FRS* Financial Reporting Standards - agreed accounting standards.

Balance sheet

> **Balance sheet:** shows the financial position of an organisation at a particular moment in time. It shows what the business owns and how this has been financed.

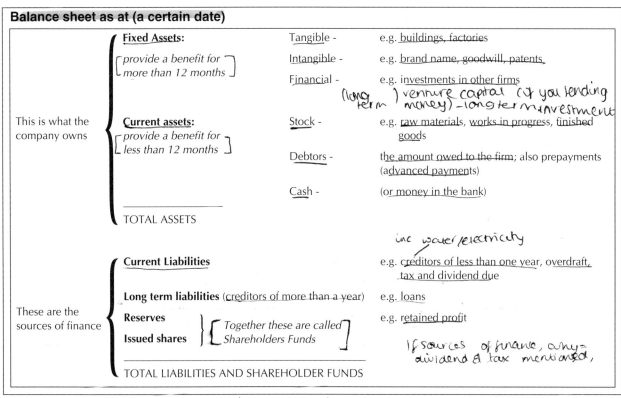

Balance sheet as at (a certain date)

This is what the company owns	**Fixed Assets:** *provide a benefit for more than 12 months*	Tangible -	e.g. buildings, factories
		Intangible -	e.g. brand name, goodwill, patents
		Financial -	e.g. investments in other firms
			(long term) venture capital (if you lending money) – long term investment
	Current assets: *provide a benefit for less than 12 months*	Stock -	e.g. raw materials, works in progress, finished goods
		Debtors -	the amount owed to the firm; also prepayments (advanced payments)
		Cash -	(or money in the bank)
	TOTAL ASSETS		

inc water/electricity

These are the sources of finance	**Current Liabilities**		e.g. creditors of less than one year, overdraft, tax and dividend due
	Long term liabilities (creditors of more than a year)		e.g. loans
	Reserves	*Together these are called Shareholders Funds*	e.g. retained profit
	Issued shares		If sources of finance, any dividend & tax mentioned,
	TOTAL LIABILITIES AND SHAREHOLDER FUNDS		

what about fixed costs ie electricity, water, wages

share capital – (venture capital)
under.

These items can be rearranged to give: ✳

Balance Sheet **as at** (a certain date)

Fixed Assets

Current assets   } *Called 'Working capital' and 'Net current assets'*

less   Current Liabilities

_____

ASSETS EMPLOYED or NET ASSETS → owned.

Long term Liabilities

Reserves   } *Together these are called Shareholders Funds*

Issued share capital

_____

CAPITAL EMPLOYED – all liabilities/sources of finance] borrowings.

CAPITAL EMPLOYED	⟶	ASSETS EMPLOYED
Sources of finance	Used to acquire	e.g. buildings, factories, stocks, cash

Balance sheet 2

Fixed assets

> FIXED ASSETS
> + CURRENT ASSETS
> = TOTAL ASSETS

A fixed asset will depreciate over time. Depreciation is the cost of a fixed asset. It is entered each year in the profit and loss account and reduces the value of the asset on the balance sheet.

If an asset is bought for £500 and it is estimated it will be sold for £100 after 4 years it will cost the firm £400. A decision must be made about how to allocate this cost. The simplest method is to allocate it in equal amounts i.e. £100 each year. This is the STRAIGHT LINE METHOD of depreciation.

Year	Value of asset on balance sheet (called Net Book Value) £	Annual cost of asset (depreciation) (appears on profit and loss) £	Accumulated depreciation £
0	500	0	0
1	400	100	100
2	300	100	200
3	200	100	300
4	100	100	400

net book value

After 2 years, value of book ↓ by £200 to value of £300.

H —
(L)
A =

Net Book Value

— Historic cost = original cost of the asset

Accumulated depreciation = total depreciation to date.

Net Book Value = historic cost - accumulated depreciation, i.e. value of asset left on balance sheet.

Residual value = value of asset at the end of its life, i.e on disposal

Brand name: intangible asset; no agreed method of valuation.

Goodwill: occurs when a firm pays more for another firm than its book value, e.g. if Firm A spends £100m buying a company worth only £90m in its accounts then £10m of 'goodwill' has been acquired. Listed as an intangible asset; represents the value of the location, skill, reputation, and management of the acquired organisation. 'Difference between the value of a business as a whole and the aggregate of a fair value of its separable net assets.'

is brand name more important so £10m goodwill to make sure you get co.

Stocks:

> appear as current assets on the balance sheet

> FIXED ASSETS
> + CURRENT ASSETS
> = TOTAL ASSETS

Should be valued at the lower of cost or net realisable value (i.e. what they would be worth if sold). Problems occur when trying to estimate what their realisable value is and when estimating their cost.

Example of problem estimating costs: A firm buys 10 units of materials in January at £30 each and another 10 units in February at £40 each. In March 10 units are used up but the firm may not know exactly which ones were used. Were they the ones bought in January or in February? If it does not know, the firm must make an assumption.

Under the FIFO principle the first in are assumed to be the first out i.e. the January materials are assumed to be used up. The cost of materials is therefore £300 (10 x £30) and the stock left is worth £400 (10 x £40).

If LIFO (last in first out) is used then it is assumed the February ones are used. The costs are therefore £400 and the stocks left are worth £300.

Some firms might assume that a mixture of January and February stocks had been used and take the average price. In which case the costs would be £350 and the stock left would be worth £350.

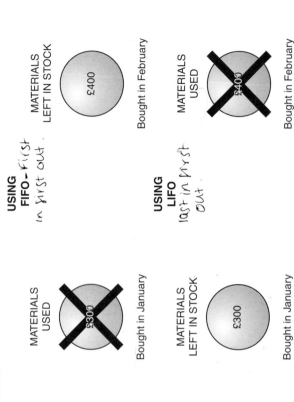

USING FIFO – first in first out.

MATERIALS USED — £300 (Bought in January)

MATERIALS LEFT IN STOCK — £400 (Bought in February)

USING LIFO – last in first out.

MATERIALS LEFT IN STOCK — £300 (Bought in January)

MATERIALS USED — £400 (Bought in February)

Debtors: appear as current assets in balance sheet

```
FIXED ASSETS
+ CURRENT ASSETS
= TOTAL ASSETS
```

balance sheet - drawback is that it does not tell you if debtors & how good they are at repaying

An analyst should try to find out more about who owes the firm money, e.g. if the money is all owed by one firm it may be riskier than if it is owed by several firms. It would also be useful to have details of the track record of the debtors, and information about how long they have owed the company money, e.g 2 days? or 11 months?

profit not shown on balance sheet.

Reserves include:

```
Issued Share capital   } Shareholders'
+ Reserves             } Funds
+ long term liabilities (or creditors for more than one year)
= CAPITAL EMPLOYED
```

Not realised - will not be actual until land sold. can use it as valuation.

*money left over spent profit on tax & dividends = retained profits. can be :
① Ploughed back into co.
② reserve (put else)*

Issued = 1st price co actually get what share premium reserve. - "share premium reserve - actual money account

- Revaluation reserves: occur when assets, such as land, increase in value. The fixed asset value is increased and to reflect the increased worth of the business a revaluation reserve is created. — *source of finance.*

- Share premium reserve: occurs when a share is issued at a price which is greater than its nominal (or face) value, e.g. if a 25p share is sold for 30p then the cash received is 30p, but the issued share capital will be recorded as 25p; the difference of 5p is listed in the share premium reserve. — *source of finance*

- Retained profits: this records the total profit the firm has made up until now. Remember that reserves are not all sitting in cash; they will also be held in other forms of assets such as stock and buildings.

Asset structure:

the proportions of various types of asset held by a firm as shown on the balance sheet, e.g. a large manufacturing company is likely to have high levels of fixed assets (e.g. equipment). Asset structure depends on:

- technology - advanced technology firms are likely to have a larger proportion of fixed assets

- the nature of the business - e.g. retailers are likely to have relatively high levels of stock. *some co's labour intensive rather than capital intensive. ↳ nursing.*

- the size of the business - e.g. small firms may not be able to afford the available technology *∴ less fixed assets.*

```
Fixed Assets
Current Assets        }
less Current Liabilities }  Working capital
_____
Net assets
```

Working capital; also called 'Net current assets':

Day to day finance of the organisation = current assets - current liabilities — *working capital.*

The management of working capital includes: *first part of product*

- minimising time lags between input of resources and payments for sold goods and services. *— final part (unless aftersales treatment)*

Not quite like JIT, but similar. →
- minimising stock levels whilst still holding enough to continue production and sales. *Means may have more money, & less to be wasted on products that could be damaged in stock, or those that have a very short PLC.*

Financial year usually April to April to fit in with tax. Fiscal year ⇒ tax year.

Pay as you earn ⇒ PAYE.

Disadvantage of goodwill - have to be better than co. before otherwise good will goes & lost.

what most people make an agreement that when co. over occurs staff stay on until gradually faced out so that customers still recognise the name & business.

macro ⇒ whole economy affected
micro ⇒ to individual.

If jar of coffee - you would write down cost as whole period (& not bother with working out how much was used in one period) & then write down it again when have to buy another jar.
Only write out % used per period for larger materials

Profit and loss statement

Profit and loss statement: shows the profit or loss generated over a given period.

It involves: **Revenue or Turnover** - this measures the value of the sales; it may not be in cash since the firm is often owed money (debtors).

Costs - this is the value of items used up in the process; this is not necessarily the same as the cash paid out; e.g. if firm pays for £300 of materials in cash but only uses up one third, the costs are £100 since the other £200 of materials remain as assets of the firm.

for large items, should only use specific goods in one period (that needed) then use up in next period.

Revenue - Direct costs = contribution (to fixed costs)

Profit and loss for the year ending 31 March 1996:

		£
Turnover		100
Less Cost of sales	cost of producing the goods/services	-40
Gross profit		60
less		
Expenses	cost of marketing, administration	-25
Operating profit		35
Non operating income	e.g. from shares in other companies	+2
Profit before interest and tax		37
Interest payable	to repay loans	-5
Profit on ordinary activities before tax (also called net profit)		32
Corporation Tax		7
Profit after tax (profit attributable to shareholders)		25
Dividends paid to shareholders		14
Retained profit		11

Retained profit - can be put in as revenues.

Other items/terms which may be listed on the profit and loss statement:

Extraordinary item: a cost or revenue which is 'out of the ordinary', i.e. not part of ordinary activities, e.g. the closure of a factory or restructuring costs.

Exceptional items: costs or revenues which are unusually large, e.g. an exceptionally large bad debt.

Balance sheet shows company worth, profit & loss shows how much it can make (revenue)... Balance sheet = only assets & valuation

---

Profit & cash

Profit is not the same as cash: e.g. If goods are sold on credit this creates revenue but no cash. If materials or equipment are bought in cash, this leads to a cash outflow, but no cost is involved until they are used up. Imagine a £450 asset is purchased for cash, is used for four years, and is then sold for £50. The overall cost is £400 (£450 - £50). Using the straight line method, the cost is £100 p.a.

Year	0	1	2	3	4
Cash flows £	(450)	0	0	0	50
Costs £ annual depreciation	0	100	100	100	100

Profit v. cash example:

A firm buys £300 of materials in cash and uses up £200 of them to produce goods which are sold on credit for £1000. Labour is paid £50 in cash. No other costs are involved.

£ ∴ cash & profit are very different.

			£
Turnover	1000	Cash in	0
Costs (labour)	50	cash out (labour)	50
(materials)	+200 →250	(materials)	300
Profit	750	Cash	(350)

Improving cashflow:

- debt factoring - a firm raises finance using its debtors as an asset. A debt factor lends cash to the firm and takes over its sales ledger, sends invoices and chases debtors. This improves a firm's cashflow, allows it to concentrate on manufacturing and selling, frees management time, and enables it to pay creditors promptly. *Though loses 20% of costs - not wise for long term.*
- increase cash sales
- give incentives for early/prompt payment ie % off
- arrange overdrafts
- use trade credit - 30 days to be paid
- use sale and leaseback - sell assets and lease them back; this raises finance whilst allowing firm to keep use of the assets. - not wise for long term.

Revenue v. Capital items

equip (asset) - don't depreciate... single item in the asset register. if for on dift on dift

Revenue items appear on the profit and loss. Capital items appear on the balance sheet. For example, a firm purchases equipment, this is an asset and appears on the balance sheet (capital item). If a firm uses up materials this is a cost and appears on the profit and loss (revenue item). Sometimes there is debate about an item, e.g. research and development. Some firms treat this as an investment, list it on the balance sheet and depreciate it over a number of years. Others 'write it off' in one year, i.e treat it as something which has been used up and so put it all as a cost in one go. (revenue item).

revenue

Ratios

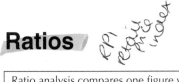

RPI / Retail price index

usually inverse relationship between shares prices & interest rates. ie price of shares ↑ when IR ↓ (bank vs IR) price of share ↓ when IR ↑ (people switch to safe environ- of bank with ↑IR.

Ratio analysis compares one figure with another to place it in context and assess its relative importance. It helps analyse data and aids decision making:

It is part of the decision making process:

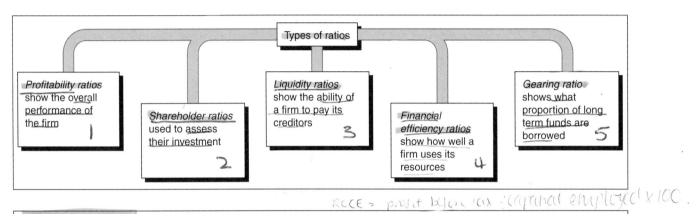

RCCE = (pre tax profit ÷ capital employed) x100. can be compared to other rates of return ie interest rates of banks.

RCCE = profit before tax ÷ capital employed x100

Profitability ratios: measure how well the firm is doing. One of the most common is *return on capital employed* (%) ROCE (profit before interest and tax ÷ capital employed) x100

Assuming firms are aiming for profit, the higher the ratio the better. It measures the rate of return being generated by managers and can be compared to other rates of return, e.g. interest rates in banks.

The overall return depends on the value of the sales and how much profit is made per sale

- The profit per sale is measured by the profit margin (%) = (profit before interest and tax ÷ sales) x100

- The value of the sales compared to the assets of the firm (i.e. the assets turnover) is measured by: sales ÷ assets employed.

Shareholder ratios

Return on equity (%) = profit attributable to ordinary shareholders ÷ ordinary share capital and reserves] x100

Shows profit attributable to ordinary shareholders compared to their investment; the higher the figure the greater the rate of return earned for shareholders.

Price/earnings ratio: The earnings are the profits of the company which could be paid out to shareholders (i.e which are attributable to ordinary shareholders). The price is the share price. The ratio measures how much investors are willing to pay for a share compared to the profits of the company per share. If this is a high figure then investors are

willing to pay more to buy the share; this suggests confidence in the future performance of the business.

Dividends per share (pence): dividends ÷ number of shares; this is the amount received by shareholders on each share.

Dividend yield (%): (dividend per share ÷ market price) x100. Shows the dividends as a rate of return compared to the price of buying a share; this should be compared with rates available elsewhere.

Dividend cover (number of times): (Profit attributable to ordinary shareholders ÷ dividends). This measures the ability of the firm to pay out dividends.

Liquidity ratios: measure the ability of an organisation to meet its short term liabilities.

Current Ratio Current asset : Current Liabilities
Typically 1.5 or 2

Acid test ratio Current assets without stocks ÷ current liabilities
(also called 'quick ratio')

The acid test is a tighter test of liquidity than the current ratio. It measures the ability of the firm to meet its current liabilities if it could not sell its stock. Usually 0.8 -1 to 1

transparency pricing

Ratios continued

Financial efficiency ratios: Show how well the firm is using its resources

Stock turnover measures the value of the firm's stock compared to its sales.

= cost of sale ÷ stocks

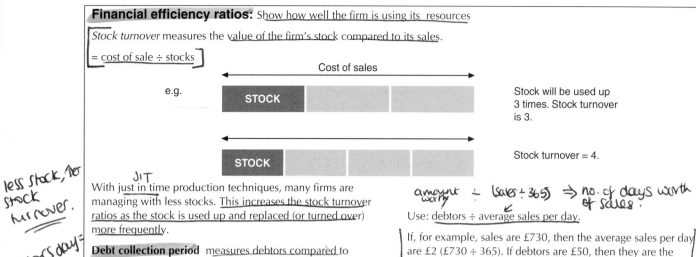

JIT

With just in time production techniques, many firms are managing with less stocks. This increases the stock turnover ratios as the stock is used up and replaced (or turned over) more frequently.

Debt collection period measures debtors compared to annual sales.

(handwritten left margin) less stock, to stock turnover. Debtors day = debtors / 365.

amount worthy ÷ (sales ÷ 365) ⇒ no. of days worth of sales.

Use: debtors ÷ average sales per day.

If, for example, sales are £730, then the average sales per day are £2 (£730 ÷ 365). If debtors are £50, then they are the equivalent of 25 days worth of sales (£50 ÷ 2).

Gearing measures how much the firm has borrowed compared to other forms of long term finance. 'Highly geared' means a high percentage of the firm's funds are borrowed.

(handwritten) As long as gearing is under 50% then the company is said to be in control of long term finance.

CAPITAL EMPLOYED

Interest cover shows how many times the profit before interest can cover the interest payments. If it is equal to 1, it means all the profits are needed to pay off the interest on debts. Generally it is 3 to 4.

borrowings

Gearing = 25%

Limitations to ratio analysis

- Ratios are only as reliable as the underlying data, i.e. if the accounts have been 'massaged' to create a favourable impression, then the ratios may also flatter. In addition, ratios are often calculated using out of date information, e.g. data from last year's accounts. Ratio analysis based on past data will not necessarily help predict the future.

- They only use quantitative data. Also need to consider qualitative factors, such as the skill of management, the rate of change in the market, and the industrial relations record.

(handwritten left margin) what do ratios mean to a particular firm

- Need to consider the type of firm, stage in its development, and the objectives of the owners, e.g a low profitability ratio may be acceptable in the early stages of growth when the owners are investing heavily in equipment and training.

- Typicality - the figures in the balance sheet show a particular day; this may not be typical and consequently any ratios calculated using these figures are not necessarily representative.

(handwritten left margin) competition in past years & firm in past years.

- Need to consider what the ratios are for other firms (inter firm comparison) and what ratios have been in the past (intra firm comparison), e.g. a 12% ROCE may seem high but it is not as impressive if others are earning 14% and last year the firm earned 16%.

- Need to consider the context, e.g. is the market growing or declining, is the economy booming or not, for example we expect profitability to be higher in a growing market.

- Usefulness depends on the skill of the user; the more experienced and able the user the more likely he or she will be to interpret the ratios effectively, place them in context, and understand their significance.

Auditors report: companies must get independent accountants to check their accounts; they produce an auditors' report. This usually states that in their opinion the annual accounts represent a 'true and fair view'.

Window dressing

Presenting accounts in a favourable manner. Window dressing is not illegal. ie massaging the figures.

The ability to window dress occurs because accounting principles can be interpreted in different ways.

Methods include :

- depreciating an asset over a longer period of time to reduce the depreciation cost per annum.

- including a valuation for brands as a fixed asset (should be reserves)

- deciding when to recognise revenue, e.g. if a company delivers a machine to a client, installs it and gives a trial period during which the client can return the machine, the revenue might be declared on delivery, after installation or after the trial period.

When analysing a firm's accounts it is important to check the Notes to the Accounts and the Statement of Accounting Policies to find out more about the way the accounts have been produced.

Why window dress?

To produce impressive results to attract investors, maintain share price, and gain favourable press coverage.

(handwritten) Shows co. in strong position – if figures were bad beforehand then shareholders could sell share & thus shares = in surplus & price drops ∴ price of co. falls.

Ratios continued

Balance Sheet — *fixed time — as soon as completed it is out of date.*

as at 17th June 1996

	£
Fixed assets	190
Current assets	
stocks	10
debtors	+ 6
cash	4 → 20
less	
Current Liabilities	10
Assets employed (or net assets)	200
issued share capital of £1 shares	100
reserves	50
long term liabilities	50
Capital Employed	200

Profit and loss for the year ending 17th June 1996

	£
turnover (or sales)	400
cost of sales	300
gross profit	100
expenses	80
operating profit	20
non operating income	0
profit before interest and tax	20
interest payable	4
tax	1
profit attributable to ordinary shareholders	15
dividends	10
retained profit	5

Turnover + cost of sales = gross profit

gross profit - expenses = operating profit.

expenses - operating profit = non operating income.

non operating income - profit before interest & tax = interest payable.

interest payable - tax = profit attributable to ordinary shareholders.

profit attributable to ordinary shareholder - dividends = retained profit.

Calculations

The shareholder ratios cannot be calculated without the share price. This cannot be found in the published accounts because it will change daily. Assume a share price of £2.00 for the calculations below.

ratio	equation	measurement	workings	answer
return on capital employed	(profit before interest and tax ÷ capital employed) × 100	%	(20 ÷ 200) × 100	10%
profit margin	(profit before interest and tax ÷ sales) × 100	%	(20 ÷ 400) × 100	5%
asset turnover	(sales ÷ assets employed)	number of times	400 ÷ 200	2
current ratio	current asset ÷ current liabilities	number of times	20 ÷ 10	2
acid test (or 'quick')	current assets without stocks ÷ current liabilities	number of times	10 ÷ 10	1
gearing	(long term liabilities ÷ capital employed) × 100	%	(50 ÷ 200) × 100	25%
interest cover	profit before interest ÷ interest	number of times	20 ÷ 4	5
stock turnover	cost of sale ÷ stock	number of times	300 ÷ 10	30
debtor days	sales ÷ 365 = sales per day / debtors ÷ sales per day	number of days worth of sales	400 ÷ 365 = £1.09 / £6 ÷ £1.09 = 5.5	5.5 days
dividend cover	profit attributed to ordinary shareholders ÷ dividend	number of times	15 ÷ 10	1.5
dividend per share	dividend ÷ number of shares	pence	10 ÷ 100	10p
dividend yield	(dividend per share ÷ market price) × 100	%	10 ÷ 200 × 100	5%
earnings per share	profit after interest and tax ÷ number of shares	pence	15 ÷ 100	15p
price earnings ratio	market share price ÷ earnings per share	number of times	200 ÷ 15	13.3
return on equity	(profit attributable to ordinary shareholders ÷ shareholders funds) × 100	%	(15 ÷ 150) × 100	10%

Break-even

Break-even is part of the decision making process. It is an aid to decision making.

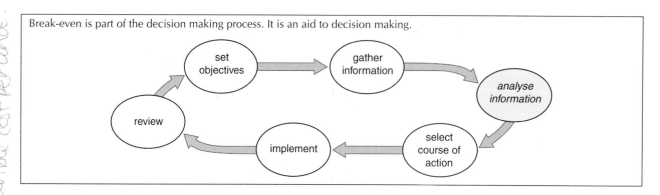

Break even is the output at which revenue equals costs, i.e. no profit or loss is made

Total costs = fixed costs + variable costs

Fixed costs do not change with output, e.g. rent; Variable costs vary directly with output, e.g. materials

Total revenue = price x quantity

Profit = total revenue - total costs

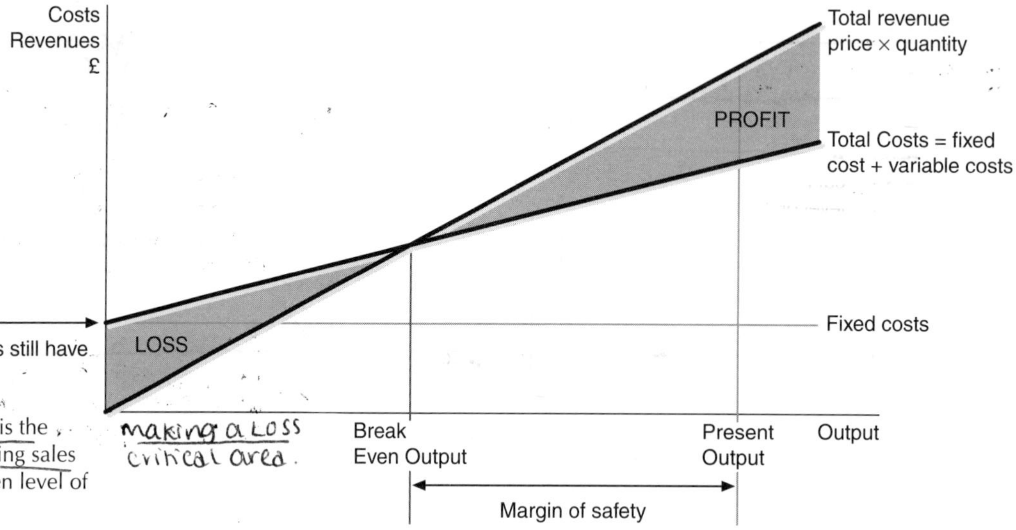

At 0 output fixed costs still have to be paid.

LOSS

PROFIT

Total revenue
price × quantity

Total Costs = fixed
cost + variable costs

Fixed costs

Costs
Revenues
£

Break
Even Output

Present
Output

Output

The *margin of safety* is the extent to which existing sales exceed the break even level of output.

making a Loss critical area.

Margin of safety

Calculating break even output:

Number of units which must be sold to break even = Fixed costs ÷ contribution per unit

Find the contribution per unit. This is selling price - variable cost per unit. This gives the contribution per unit towards fixed costs. Find how many units must be sold for these contributions to cover fixed costs.

Example: Price per unit £10; Variable cost per unit £4; Fixed Costs £12000; maximum output 5000 units.

Contribution per unit = £10 - £4= £6

Fixed costs/contribution = £12000 ÷ £6 = 2000 units, i.e. 2000 units must be sold to get a large enough contribution to meet the fixed costs.

Plotting the break even graph: produce a table which calculates Total costs and Total revenue.

Example: Price per unit £10; Variable cost per unit £4; Fixed Costs £12000; maximum output 5000 units.

Quantity	Revenue (price × quantity) £	Fixed Costs £	Variable costs (variable cost per unit × quantity) £	Total costs £	Profit/loss £
0	0	12000	0	12000	(12000)
1000	10000	12000	4000	16000	(6000)
2000	20000	12000	8000	20000	0-break even
5000	50000	12000	20000	32000	18000

Handwritten margin notes (left side, vertical): Fixed costs - contribution per unit. Contribution per unit → measurement of inflation. Retail price interest. Revenue - Direct costs. Selling price - variable cost per unit.

pan European strategy ⇒ global, efficient, gives global image.
can't cater for local, many culture.
diff - some words don't fit.

Plotted from previous table:

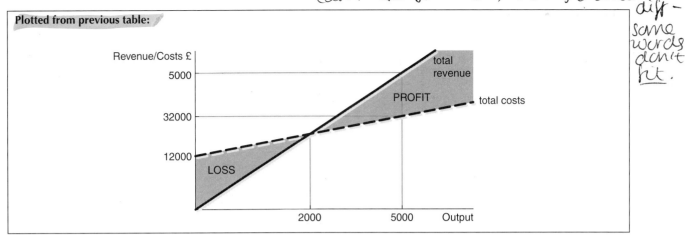

- Revenue/Costs £
- 5000
- 32000
- 12000
- LOSS
- PROFIT
- total revenue
- total costs
- 2000
- 5000
- Output

Break-even helps the firm to analyse what happens if:

- output is changed
- price is changed
- variable costs are changed
- fixed costs are changed

but does not take into consideration, what people want - elasticity of product

---

Limitations of break-even:

- assumes all the output is sold; in fact sales may not equal output

- assumes output is all sold at one price; in reality the firm may have to lower price to sell more

- assumes variable costs are constant per unit; in reality they may vary with discounts or changes in productivity *or rin IR making products more expensive (raw materials)*

- only as useful as the underlying data; if data is out of date, it has limited usefulness; usefulness depends on the skill and experience of the user

⇒ good for model, but very limited to real life — some products would not be bought if price went up ⇒ convenience goods.

A
cut in variable costs, at any level of output more profit is made but will quality and sales suffer?

- Revenue/Costs £
- Total Revenue
- Total Cost₁
- Total Cost₂
- Break even₂
- Break even₁
- Output

Rent can be variable ∴ more products made, might need more room for expanding ∴ price goes up.

Different scenarios where break even looks good & high profit margin will be made - but haven't looked at external factors - gov, customers.

B
increase price so more revenue for every level of sales but how much will sales fall?

- Revenue/Costs £
- Total Revenue₂
- Total Revenue₁
- Total Costs
- Break even₂
- Break even₁
- Output

C
cut fixed costs but only possible in long run and may be difficult too e.g. reduce factory space.

- Revenue/Costs £
- Total Revenue
- Total Cost₁
- Total Cost₂
- Break even₂
- Break even₁
- Output

↑ lower margin of safety (B₂) & costs ↑ ∴ bigger profit margin - but will the customers bear this extra cost - depends on product & how co. markets it.

lower margin of safety

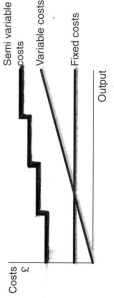

Revenue - Direct cost -)
Prop. of fixed costs*

(Prod-/quantity)
=> contribution per bottle towards fixed costs.

	Prod ('000)	Direct costs	Revenue
Wine A	90	100000	120 000
B	50	80 000	100 000
	40	60 000	+ 150 000
			370000

Fixed costs = 80000
(contribution per bottle)
(contribution to fixed costs)
(Revenue - Direct costs): Prod

Allocate fixed costs as direct result of revenue
120000/370000 × 100000 =
100000/370000 × 100000 =
150000/370000 × 100000 =

If production of A ↑ would it affect others at direct costs

vary with activity: to capture on A would be B least double

means more responsibility (govt involvement/encouragement): per motivation.

Costing

Measuring costs

Cost centre: a business unit to which costs are allocated. It may be an individual, division, product or region. The measurement of costs for different units enables management to keep control and make better decisions as well as providing employees with targets which are relevant to their particular area of the business.

Profit centre: a business unit to which costs and revenues are allocated. It may be an individual, division, product or region.

Types of costs

Variable costs: change directly with output, e.g. raw materials

Fixed costs do not change with output, e.g. rent

Semi variable costs vary with output but not directly, e.g. supervision costs, maintenance costs, electricity & water unless fixed per month.

[Graph labelled: Costs £ (vertical axis), Output (horizontal axis); lines for Semi variable costs, Variable costs, Fixed costs]

Direct costs: costs which can be identified with a particular cost centre (e.g a product or process) and which vary directly with activity or output, e.g. the materials used in one process or labour directly involved in one product

Indirect costs: costs which cannot be directly identified with a particular cost centre, e.g. general marketing costs or administration. Also called **overheads.**

Indirect costs may be fixed (e.g rent) or variable (e.g variable overheads such as maintenance costs; these are not directly associated with a cost centre, and, although more maintenance is likely to be needed with expansion, these costs will not change directly with output).

ie tax on prod. from outside UK

VAT - value added tax - consumer not aware of it.

Absorption costing:
is based on the same idea as full costing but does not allocate all indirect costs using the same rule. Different allocation rules are used for different types of indirect costs, e.g.

Rent may be apportioned on the basis of the area occupied by each cost centre.

Heating costs may be apportioned on the basis of the amount of space taken up by a given centre.

Insurance costs may be apportioned on the basis of value of assets in each centre. (inc. humans)

Advantages of full and absorption costing:
- makes managers aware of the total cost of a product
- provides a full cost to enable a suitable price to be set, i.e a price which will cover all costs and ensure a profit

BUT

- the costs may be apportioned in different ways which will give different results; there is no set way of apportioning costs and changing the rule will give different results for each cost centre.

It is important to remember that many of the indirect costs must be paid whether or not a particular product is produced.

	A £	B £	C £
Turnover	100	50	40
Direct costs	60	30	10
Indirect costs	50	5	5
Profit/loss	(10)	15	25

Although product A makes a loss, it makes a contribution of 40 (£100- £60) towards indirect costs. if the firm stopped producing A many of the £50 of indirect costs would now have to be covered by the other products, e.g the rent of the factory will not stop just because one type of product is no longer made. In the short run, at least, production of A should continue. In the long run it might be possible to reduce indirect costs, e.g sell/lease out part of the factory space.

Marginal costing/Contribution costing:
Contribution= revenue - variable costs

Fixed costs are left unallocated. The contribution of each centre is calculated. This contributes towards the fixed costs.

£	Product A	Product B	Product C	Total
Revenue	100	60	30	190
Variable costs	60	30	10	100
Contribution	40	30	20	90

Revenue - (fixed + variable (cost)) = profit

	£
Total contribution	90
Fixed costs	60
Profit	30

Revenue - variable cost = contribution

Contribution costing useful for deciding whether to accept one off orders (known as 'special order decisions'): provided the order makes a positive contribution towards indirect costs it will increase profits or reduce losses.

Full costing:
overheads are divided (apportioned) between the various cost centres. Firms have to decide on an allocation rule. In the example below, indirect costs of £60 have been apportioned in the ratio 60% : 30% : 10% i.e the same proportion as direct costs.

	A £	B £	C £
Turnover	100	50	40
Direct costs	60	30	10
Indirect costs	50	5	5
Profit/loss	(10)	15	25

Budgeting

A budget is a quantitative statement which covers a specific period and is usually expressed in financial terms.

Budgets:

Makes sure got everything thought through.

- help planning

- help coordinate different activities so that, e.g. overall costs are not too high

- allocate responsibilities and communicate to subordinates what they have to achieve

- motivate employees by setting targets

- enable superiors to review performance by referring back to the set budget at the end of the period.

Types of budget:

Sales budget: sets sales estimates for each product in terms of number of units

Production budget: sets output targets

Cash budget: cash flow forecast

Master budget: summarises estimated income, expenditure, and profit.

Fixed and flexible budgets: A fixed budget gives a target for a given level of activity, e.g. costs of £1000 for 200 units. A flexible budget shows figures at different levels of activity, e.g. costs for different *levels of output*.

Zero based budgeting: before a budget is set for any activity it is critically reviewed. The assumption is that there will be no money available; managers then have to justify why they should have a budget.

Budgetary control: the difference between the forecasted figure in the budget and the actual figure is called the variance.

Positive or favourable variance: occurs when actual costs are lower than forecasted or revenue is higher; i.e. profits are higher than expected.

Negative or adverse variance: occurs when actual costs are higher than expected or revenue is lower .i.e profits are lower than expected.

Item	Budgeted	Actual	Variance
Sales of product A	100 units	120 units	POSITIVE - should increase profit
Direct Labour costs	£300	£350	NEGATIVE - should decrease profit
Indirect costs	£400	£350	POSITIVE - should increase profit

Causes of variances:

Quantity variances (i.e. actual sales differ from forecasts) could be due to:

economic climate/marketing efforts/competitor's actions

Labour variance due to direct labour efficiency or wage rates e.g absenteeism/ rise in wages/ poor supervision/

Even if got a product making a loss if its contribution to indirect costs is high it is worthwhile to keep it running as rent will not decrease if one product is not being made - unless parts can be sold / leased off. Depends.

Herzberg 2 factor theory ⇒ Hygiene & motivators.

5 - physiological needs.
4 - safety
3 - social
2 - self esteem
1 - self actualisation/fulfilment

Investment

Investment appraisal: assessing the attractiveness of different capital projects. These projects usually involve a high level of expenditure and cannot be easily reversed. They involve a high degree of risk. Investment may be in factories or plant or equipment.

It is part of the decision making process:

Set objectives - gather information - *analyse information* - select course of action - implement - review.

When considering an investment a firm will consider:
- the initial cost
- the expected benefits and costs
- the risk involved
- the alternatives

Methods of investment appraisal

Payback:

This is the length of time it takes for the firm to recoup its initial investment.

Average rate of return (ARR):

This is the average profit per year as a percentage of the initial investment.

(average return p.a. ÷ initial cost) x 100

Net Present Value:

This method takes account of the 'time value of money'. £1 in a year's time is not as desirable as £1 now; £1 in five year's time is even less desirable - firms would prefer to have the money today. Therefore when firms estimate the expected inflows an investment project will bring in the future, these figures must be discounted (reduced) to calculate what they are worth today, i.e. their present values. *Discount factors are used to calculate a discounted cash flow.*

e.g. Year Discount factor

1 0.909 - this means the firm thinks that £1 in one year's time is equal to 90.9p now

2 0.826- this means the firm thinks that £1 in 2 year's time is equal to 82.6p now

---

EXAMPLE:

Year	£	Discount factors	Calculation	Present value
0	(200)	1	(200) × 1	(200)
1	50	0.909	50 × 0.909	45.45
2	50	0.826	50 × 0.826	41.3
3	100	0.751	100 × 0.751	75.1
4	160	0.683	160 × 0.683	109.28

Payback = 3 years

(£50 in year 1 + £50 in year 2 + £100 year 3 = £200 initial outflow)

Average rate of return = 20%

Calculation:

total inflows = 50 + 50 + 100 + 160 = £360
initial cost = 200
overall return = net inflows - initial cost
= £360 - £200 = £160

average return per year = overall return ÷ number of years
= £160 ÷ years = £40 p.a

average rate of return = (average return per year ÷ initial cost) x100 = (40 ÷ 200)x100 = 20%

net present value:

The present value of the future expected inflows = £45.45 + £41.3 + £75.1 + 109.28 = £271.13. This what the firm believes the future earnings of the project are worth in today's terms.
The initial outflow = £200
Net present value = discounted inflows - initial outflow
= £271.13 - £200
= £71.13

In today's terms the project is expected to be worth £71.13 more than its cost therefore, it is worth investing. The higher the net present value, the more the project is worth compared to its cost.

The discount rate depends on factors such as the interest rate, expected inflation, and risk. If the interest rate is high, firms would rather have the money now than later so future inflows are discounted more than if the interest rate is low.
If the project is high risk and the value of money is expected to be much lower in the future, the firm will again discount future expected earnings to a greater extent.

Limitations of investment appraisal:

- only considers quantitative factors. Ignores qualitative factors such as employee and community reaction to any proposal.

- only as reliable as the data. Because some of the calculations are complicated, it is tempting to think they are correct. In fact the figures are all based on expectations and so cannot be guaranteed.

- skill of the user. The usefulness depends on how well managers can use these techniques and interpret the results.

Opportunity cost:

Opportunity cost: the cost of the next best alternative; if, for example, a firm invests in a new promotional campaign, then the money and resources used for this could have been used for something else, e.g. new equipment. When considering an investment, a manager should always consider what is being sacrificed, i.e. the opportunity cost.

Internal and external costs and benefits

When assessing a project, a firm will usually consider its internal (or 'private') costs and benefits, such as the cost of labour, rent, equipment, and the revenue from sales. These are the financial costs and benefits it will pay or receive and which affect its financial accounts. Firms do not usually include the 'external effects' of what they do, e.g. the effect on the environment or the impact on the community. To find the cost or benefit of any action to society as a whole (rather than just to the firm) the external effects should be included.

Social costs = internal costs + external costs
Social benefits = internal benefits + external benefits

Cost benefit analysis

An investment appraisal technique which attempts to measure the social costs and benefits of a project, not just the private costs and benefits. It would, for example, try to estimate the 'external cost' of a motorway in terms of the pollution, the noise and damage to wildlife. Often used by the Government but it can be difficult to quantify external costs and benefits.

Cash flow

Cash is a tangible money asset. It is shown in the current assets on the balance sheet. Cash flow statements show the flows of cash into and out of the business. Cash flow forecasts attempt to predict flows to highlight when cash might have to be borrowed or when it could be invested.

Cash flow forecasts

Example:
Opening balance is £1050

Sales for January, February and March are £300, £600 and £1200. One third is paid in cash; the remainder is paid one month later.

Materials each month are £300 paid for in cash. Wages are £200 in cash each month. rent is paid 3 months at a time in January, April, July and October. It is £600 for three months.

Opening balance - amount the firm starts the period with

£	January	February	March
Opening balance	1050	50	(50)
Cash in			
cash sales	100	200	400
credit sales	-	200	400
Cash out			
materials	300	300	300
wages	200	200	200
rent	600	-	-
Closing balance	50	(50)	250

Cash inflows - e.g. some of this period's sales may be paid in cash; also cash might be paid from previous credit sales

Cash outflows - e.g. cash payments this month on labour or materials

Closing balance - amount of cash left at the end of the period. This becomes the opening balance for next period.

Cashflow statements

Companies now have to produce a cashflow statement on their accounts. Under FRS 1 1991 this replaces the Funds Flow Statement in published accounts. It will look something like this:

Cashflow statement for the year ending 17th June 1996

	£
Net cash inflow from operating activities	
Returns on investment:	**2800**
interest received	*700*
interest paid	*(400)*
dividends paid	*(800)*
Net cash inflow from returns on investment and servicing of finance	**(500)**
Taxations - corporation tax paid	**(500)**
Investing activities	
purchase of tangible fixed asset	(810)
investments made	(40)
disposal of tangible fixed assets	50
Net cash outflow from investing activities	**(800)**
Net cash inflow/ (outflow) before financing	**1000**
Financing:	
Issue of ordinary share capital	100
Repay loans	(300)
Net cash outflow from financing	**(200)**
Increase in cash and cash equivalents	**800**

(Small limited companies do not have to publish a cashflow statement.)

Operations management

Types of production
- *Primary:* extractive industries, e.g coal mining
- *Secondary:* manufacturing sector, e.g carmakers
- *Tertiary:* services, e.g travel agents

The UK has a small primary sector and has a growing tertiary sector.

	%	
1995	3.9	Primary
	28.4	Secondary
	67.7	Tertiary

Methods of production
- Job   one off or project production, e.g building a dam or a ship
- Batch   items are produced in 'batches', i.e they all undergo one operation before being moved onto the next operation, e.g baking bread
- Flow   continuous production process; each unit moves from one operation onto the next without waiting for a batch to be completed.
- Mass   large scale production

Research and development
(R & D) To be competitive firms need to research into new ideas and develop these ideas into products. R & D may be undertaken by firms themselves or bought in from e.g universities. R & D represents an investment for the long term. It is a vital source of new ideas, innovation and competitive advantage. UK firms are often criticised for not undertaking enough research and development.

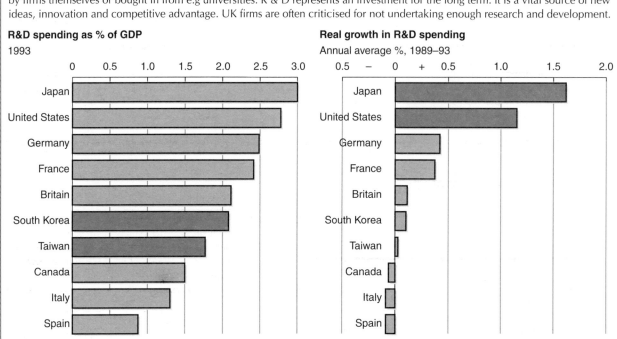

R&D spending as % of GDP 1993

Real growth in R&D spending Annual average %, 1989–93

Value analysis: each aspect of a product is examined to see if costs could be reduced without affecting the value placed on the final good by the consumer.

Work study (Taylor's approach to job design): examination of work to improve methods and establish suitable standards to assess performance.

Involves:
Method study - systematic process of recording and analysing existing and proposed methods of doing work to develop more effective and easier methods.

Work measurement - techniques to establish the time for a qualified worker to carry out a job at a given level of performance.

Subcontracting: using other producers to meet an order. Why ? To make use of specialist skills; because a firm is at full capacity and cannot meet the order, because it may be cheaper. Consider: the subcontractors' reliability, price and quality.

Idle time: occurs when the production process is not operational, e.g broken down or waiting for materials to arrive or machines being retooled (reset) to produce a new product. Also called 'downtime'.

Productivity: <u>OUTPUT</u>
                 INPUT

Productivity can be increased by: training, higher motivation, more capital equipment

Capacity: the amount the firm can produce

Capacity utilisation:
the percentage of productive capacity which is being used, e.g. a capacity utilisation of 50% means half of its productive capacity is being used.

Overcapacity:
the maximum capacity of producers is greater than the demand; often leads to price cutting and very competitive market.

Automation: use of machines to replace employees; leads to transfers or redundancies.

CNC: computer numerically controlled machines, e.g. for cutting and shaping metal.

CAM: (computer aided manufacture) use of computers to support the manufacturing process.

Flexible manufacturing system: (FMS) automated production system which can manufacture a wide range of products.

Technology

CAD: (computer aided design) use of computers to assist in the production of designs and drawings and data for use in the manufacturing process.

Computer integrated manufacture: (CIM) use of information technology to integrate various elements of manufacturing process, e.g design and production.

Manufacturing resource planning: (MRP II) computerised, planning system for production. Turns sales forecasts into purchasing requirements for materials,components, and production scheduling. Coordinates all the various orders into a production schedule which attempts to maximise capacity utilisation. Can be used to answer 'what if' questions, e.g. what are the implications of increasing output by 5%?

Modern production techniques

- *Cellular production:* small number of closely cooperating machines; equipment is grouped to produce parts which are then moved to the next cell.

- *kaizen:* (continuous improvement); an approach which stresses that improvement can come from small and gradual developments; seeks to establish a continuous process of improvement through discussion and review

- *Lean production:* waste saving measures such as Just in Time production and shorter product development times.

- *Time as a competitive advantage:* firms can gain a competitive edge by developing products more quickly (shorter product development times) and delivering more quickly.

Just in time production: firms produce 'just in time' when goods or service are ordered. They do not hold stocks.

Advantages
- Minimises stock holding costs
- Money not tied up
- Focuses effort on quality as finished goods sent to customer immediately not left in stock

Disadvantages
- May not be able to meet sudden increase in demand
- Very reliant on suppliers and employees
- May lose bulk buying discounts
- Vulnerable to breakdowns

Choosing suppliers: depends on the quality, the reliability, when they can deliver and the price. In the past firms tended to use many suppliers and switch from one to the other depending on which one offered the lowest price. Firms tended to 'bully' suppliers to get the price down. The modern approach is to use fewer suppliers and build long term, cooperative relationships with them.

Location

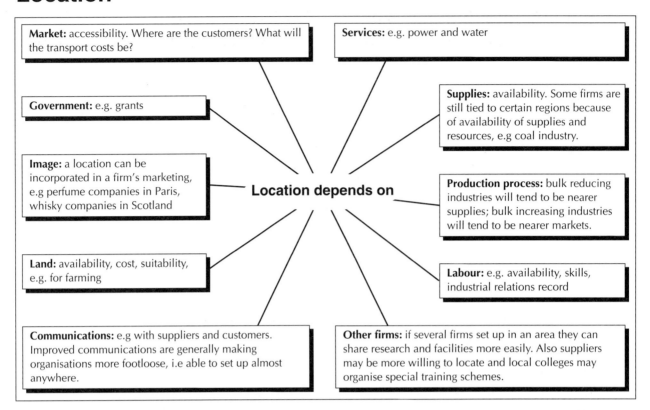

Market: accessibility. Where are the customers? What will the transport costs be?

Services: e.g. power and water

Government: e.g. grants

Supplies: availability. Some firms are still tied to certain regions because of availability of supplies and resources, e.g coal industry.

Image: a location can be incorporated in a firm's marketing, e.g perfume companies in Paris, whisky companies in Scotland

Production process: bulk reducing industries will tend to be nearer supplies; bulk increasing industries will tend to be nearer markets.

Location depends on

Land: availability, cost, suitability, e.g. for farming

Labour: e.g. availability, skills, industrial relations record

Communications: e.g with suppliers and customers. Improved communications are generally making organisations more footloose, i.e able to set up almost anywhere.

Other firms: if several firms set up in an area they can share research and facilities more easily. Also suppliers may be more willing to locate and local colleges may organise special training schemes.

Industrial inertia: firms stay in an area even if the original reason for locating there has gone.

Greenfield site: location which has no previous experience of a given type of industry.

Government assistance

Regional assistance is available in Development Areas and Intermediate Areas which are regions of severe economic decline.

- Selective Regional Assistance - discretionary grant towards capital and training costs.

- Regional Enterprise Grants - firms with fewer than 25 employees in Development Areas can gain investment grants or grants towards innovation or new process.

- Enterprise Zones - inner city areas; financial incentives offered to firms to locate here, e.g subsidised premises.

- Local Authority help - advice and grants for firms.

- Department of Trade and Industry - has an Investment in Britain Bureau to attract inward investment by overseas firms.

- European Union - also offers help for depressed areas via the European Regional Development Fund (money for infrastructure e.g roads) and the European Social Fund (money for training).

Stocks

Raw materials, works in progress, finished goods. Stocks appear as current assets on the balance sheet.

The aim of stock control is to hold sufficient quantities and quality of stock to enable production and sales to continue whilst minimising costs.

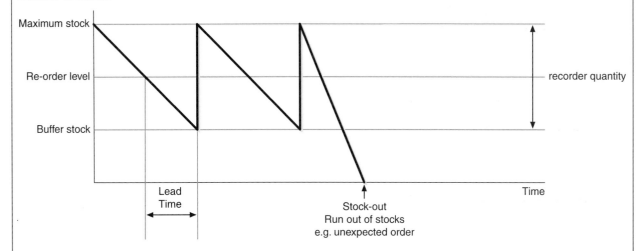

Reorder level: level of stocks at which new supplies are ordered

Reorder quantity: amount reordered

Buffer stock: safety stock in case of sudden increases in demand or supply failure

Lead time: time taken from ordering supplies to supplies arriving

---

The level of stocks held by a firm will depend on:
- the nature of the product, e.g. is the good perishable?
- suppliers, e.g. how often do they deliver? how reliable are they?
- the facilities available, e.g. warehouse space
- stockholding costs, e.g. insurance and security
- management policies, e.g. just in time production reduces stock levels.

Cost of holding stocks:
- warehousing costs
- insurance and security costs
- stocks may depreciate
- opportunity costs - stocks tie up money which could be used elsewhere
- theft.

Too little stock:
- Production may not be possible - may lead to down-time and idle labour
- May not be able to meet orders - lose customer loyalty; dissatisfied customers may tell others

---

Kanban (= visible records): A 'pull' system of stock control. Parts or components are ordered and pulled through the production process only when needed. This is different from the traditional approach where stocks are made in advance, ready for production.

Quality

To achieve high quality, a good or service must be 'fit for the purpose' and 'meet customer requirements'. The term customer is now broadly used to mean customers inside and outside of the business i.e internal and external customers. Anyone an employee does work for should be regarded as a customer.

Costs of poor quality:
dissatisfied customers/goods have to reworked or thrown away/may have to replace items or give refund/may be sued/wasted materials.

Benchmarking:
used by some organisations to discover best practices in other firms. Identify best practices (best ways of doing things) in other firms and measure own performance against these; it involves learning how to improve from others.

Traditional and modern views of quality:
Traditional quality control involved inspection at the end of the production line. When a good or service was produced, it would be inspected to find the faults. Nowadays the aim is to prevent faults occurring in the first place, i.e. the emphasis is on prevention rather than inspection, e.g. preventative maintenance to prevent faults occurring rather than fixing them once they have occurred.

Quality assurance:
implementing quality systems to ensure that quality standards will be met to ensure customer satisfaction. Involves checking that standards are met within the firm. Quality assurance emphasises preventing defects whereas quality control focuses on detecting faults once they have occurred. Quality assurance seeks to build quality into the system.

Deming: major writer on quality. Deming's 14 points include:

- Create a constancy of purpose towards improvement of product and service.
- Find problems. Constantly improve.
- Cease dependence on inspection. Seek evidence that quality is built in.

Total quality management:
Systematic method of ensuring all activities happen in the way they have been planned and meet customer requirements.

- quality is the responsibility of every employee not just the quality control department

- every employee is empowered to take action if quality is not acceptable

- employees should regard all people they work for and deal with as customers

- the target is zero defects

- all procedures must be monitored to ensure they meet the set standards

- employees should work in teams to share skills and ideas

But involves training costs and requires total commitment from management

Crosby's absolutes:
- The definition of quality is CONFORMANCE TO REQUIREMENTS (i.e. meet customer requirements).

- The system of quality is PREVENTION (i.e. stop mistakes happening).

- The performance standard is ZERO DEFECTS (i.e. no errors allowed)

- The measurement of quality is the PRICE OF NON CONFORMANCE (i.e. consider the cost of getting it wrong).

Statistical process control techniques: detect
and help to eliminate non random variation in the production process. An upper and lower limit is set; samples are taken and results monitored, e.g. desired weight might be 100g; upper limit 100.5g; lower limit 99.5g.

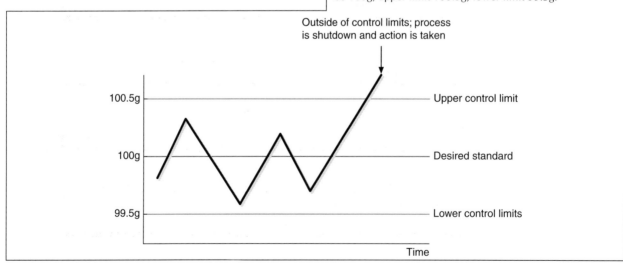

Quality standards:
BS 5750 and ISO 9000 - quality accreditation standard. To gain this award organisations must have suitable policies, procedures and practices to ensure they meet their own quality standards.

Human resource planning

Human resource management: regards people as an important resource of the organisation which needs to be managed effectively.

People add value to the organisation by:

- increasing productivity
- improving quality
- innovating
- improving customer service

INPUTS $\longrightarrow$ PEOPLE ADD VALUE $\longrightarrow$ OUTPUTS

People can differentiate one organisation from another and are an important source of competitive advantage. Human resource management aims to enhance the contribution of individuals and groups towards the organisational objectives now and in the future.

This involves:

- attracting the right numbers of employees with the right skills and attitudes
- developing individuals to meet the challenges of their jobs now and in the future

- providing a safe and healthy environment in which to work
- enabling employees to contribute to the organisation
- developing an environment in which people are used to their full capacity and potential

Human resource management is a 'staff' function (i.e advisory); it seeks to enable managers to manage their own employees more effectively.

Indicators of effective human resource management:

- low labour turnover: measured by (number of employees leaving in given period ÷ average number employed) x 100, e.g. 12 leave out of 50 = 12 ÷ 50 x 100 = 24% labour turnover.
- high productivity (measured by output per worker)
- low wastage rates
- low scrap rates (i.e. relatively few products scrapped or reworked)

- good industrial relations
- cooperative workforce
- better customer service
- high quality production

Investors in People: Government award for firms which train and develop their employees.

Human resource planning: systematic process of planning human resource requirements for the organisation.

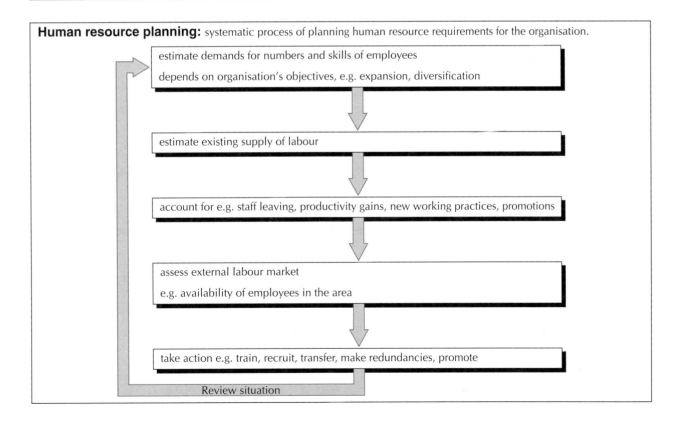

estimate demands for numbers and skills of employees

depends on organisation's objectives, e.g. expansion, diversification

estimate existing supply of labour

account for e.g. staff leaving, productivity gains, new working practices, promotions

assess external labour market

e.g. availability of employees in the area

take action e.g. train, recruit, transfer, make redundancies, promote

Review situation

Recruitment and selection

Hiring a new employee is an investment; it is important to get the right person for the right job. The right person will add value to an organisation; the wrong person can increase costs and reduce quality. Organisations can never be sure that they have selected the right person until he or she starts work, but an effective recruitment and selection process can reduce the risk.

Recruitment and selection process:

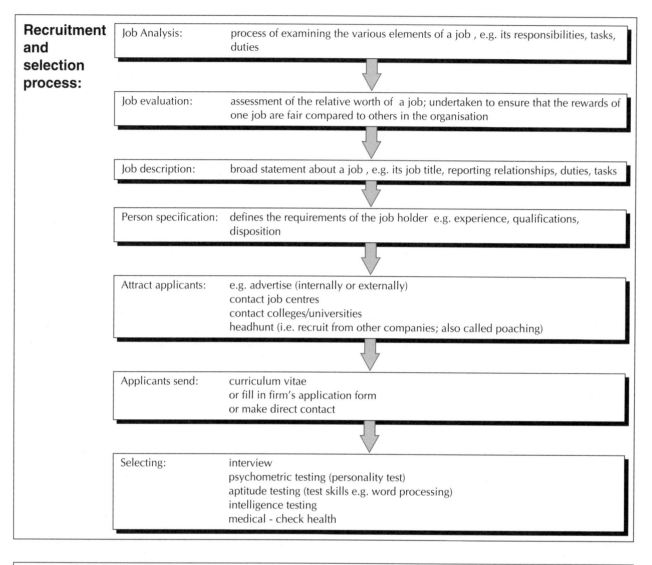

Job Analysis: process of examining the various elements of a job , e.g. its responsibilities, tasks, duties

Job evaluation: assessment of the relative worth of a job; undertaken to ensure that the rewards of one job are fair compared to others in the organisation

Job description: broad statement about a job , e.g. its job title, reporting relationships, duties, tasks

Person specification: defines the requirements of the job holder e.g. experience, qualifications, disposition

Attract applicants:
e.g. advertise (internally or externally)
contact job centres
contact colleges/universities
headhunt (i.e. recruit from other companies; also called poaching)

Applicants send:
curriculum vitae
or fill in firm's application form
or make direct contact

Selecting:
interview
psychometric testing (personality test)
aptitude testing (test skills e.g. word processing)
intelligence testing
medical - check health

Advantages of recruiting:

Internally
- know the employee already
- employee knows organisation already
- may be quicker
- may be cheaper
- motivates employees

Externally
- more choice
- can benefit from the experience of employees who have worked for other firms.

When recruiting consider:
- how much time is available before vacancy has to be filled?
- how much money should be/can be spent?
- what is most effective means of attracting applicants, e.g. unlikely to advertise nationally for a very junior post
- what is the state of the labour market?
- what is an appropriate reward package?

Assessing the effectiveness of the recruitment and selection process:
- Ratios, e.g. number of applicants : number manager felt were suitable to be interviewed
- Performance in the job once recruited
- Cost
- Time taken
- Retention rates, i.e. how long do people stay once they have been recruited?

Employment

Offering the job: employees are entitled to a written contract of employment within 13 weeks of starting work. It includes: job title, rate of pay and method of pay, normal	hours of work, holiday arrangements, sick pay and pension arrangements, disciplinary and grievance procedures, and the length of notice due to and from the employee.

Training

Induction training: introduces employees to their job and the organisation as a whole, e.g history, mission, rules

On the job training: employees learn whilst undertaking the job;

Off the job training: employees trained away from the actual job; may be within firm or at outside college.

Training and Enterprise Councils: organise training in their regions

The value of training:

- increases employees' skills in their present jobs
- prepares employees for change
- increases the organisations flexibility
- motivates employees
- can reduce mistakes and improve profits.

Appraisal: assessing an employee's performance in his or her job. This should be an ongoing process but some organisations also have a formal appraisal process. Used to identify training needs.

Policies and procedures

Grievance procedure: process by which employees can complain about the way in which they are treated

Discipline procedure: process by which employees are disciplined, e.g verbal warning, written warning, final written warning and dismissal.

Equal opportunities policy: provides employees with the same opportunities regardless of race or colour or gender, i.e. does not discriminate.

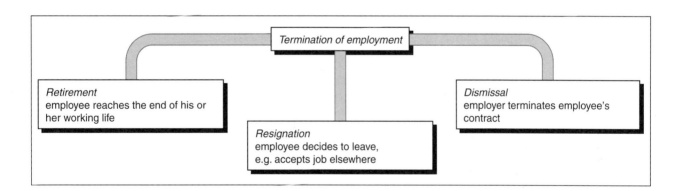

Dismissal

Fair dismissal: termination of an individual's employment contract for a fair reason according to the law.

Fair reasons include:

- illegality, e.g. employee lied about qualifications
- incapability - employee is incapable of doing the work
- job no longer exists (redundancy)
- any other substantial reason, e.g. physical assault

Unfair dismissal: the reason for the termination of employment is regarded as unfair in law, e.g. cannot dismiss someone for being a member of a union or for being pregnant.

Constructive dismissal: the organisation creates a situation in which the employee feels he or she has to resign, e.g. because of harassment.

Summary dismissal: employee dismissed on the spot without a further warning. Only occurs when there has been a severe breach of the organisation's rules (called 'gross misconduct').

If employees feel they have been unfairly dismissed or discriminated against, they can appeal to an *industrial tribunal;* this is an industrial court which judges whether or not the employer behaved fairly.

Employment continued

Redundancy: employee is made redundant because of the closure of all or part of the business. An employee who has worked full time for the organisation for more than two years or part time for five years is entitled to statutory redundancy pay. (Full time is defined as more than 16 hours per week). Firms may pay more than the legal requirement.

Outplacement services: are provided by some firms to help employees find alternative employment. May involve information, advice and the provision of various facilities (e.g. reference books, newspapers, word processors).

Issues with redundancy:
Employers must consider:
- which jobs to cut
- how to select employees
- the amount of notice to be given
- the degree of consultation
- redundancy payments

Voluntary redundancy: occurs when individuals are willing to be made redundant (i.e. they volunteer for it).

Employment patterns

Changes in the UK labour market in the 1980s and 1990s:
- older population
- less younger people entering workforce
- more women workers
- more part time workers
- more jobs in the service sector
- more flexible working patterns

Flexible working patterns:
- flexitime: employees have some freedom over what hours they work
- temporary workers: employees work for a few days or a few weeks at a time
- multi-skilling: employees trained in a variety of tasks
- homeworking: working at home, e.g. telecommuting - working via computer
- part time jobs: employees work a few hours each week
- job sharing: two or more people share job, e.g. one works mornings, another works afternoons.
- removal of job demarcation (demarcation line defines the tasks involved in one job; by removing these employees can undertake more tasks)

Flexible working patterns:
- allow firms to increase or decrease their output more easily. This means that firms can match supply to demand more effectively
- allow individuals to develop work patterns which suit their own lifestyles e.g. part time work whilst raising children.

Employment type	1985 %	1995 %	2005 (estimated) %
Permanent	84	82	79
Part time	21	24	25
Self employed	11	13	13.5
Temporary	5	6	8

Source: Business Strategies

Unions

Represent, protect, inform, and provide services for employees on a factory, local, and national level.

Types of unions:

- craft - for employees with a particular skill, e.g. electricians AEEU
- industry - for employees in particular industry, e.g. coalminers NUM
- general - broad union for wide range of employees usually unskilled or semi-skilled, e.g. TGWU
- white collar - for clerical, professional or managerial staff, e.g. NUT (teachers)
- staff associations for employees in a particular organisation, e.g. Marks and Spencer

Union recognition: occurs when an employer agrees to bargain with a union over, e.g. wages. Employers do not have to recognise unions but employees cannot be prevented from joining a union.

Industrial relations: the state of the relationship between employer, unions and employees.

Benefits of unions

To employers
- channel of communication
- can highlight human resource implications of any action
- provide ideas/ information

To employees
- provide power
- provide advice
- provide services, e.g. legal advice if dismissed
- provide protection

Employees' views of what a trade union should try to do:

	1994 %
protect existing jobs	37
improve working conditions	20
improve pay	15
have more say over management's long term plans	14
have more say over how work is done day to day	5
reduce pay differences at the workplace	4
work for equal opportunities for women	2

Source: British Attitudes Survey, Social and Community Planning Research

Consultation with unions
managers ask union representatives for their opinions; managers make final decision

v.

Bargaining with unions
managers negotiate with unions; final decision depends on negotiation

Collective bargaining: union representative negotiates on behalf of a group of employees. Employees have more power as they are bargaining as a group rather than individually.

Forms of industrial action:

- overtime ban - can make it difficult for a firm to meet its orders
- sit in - employees occupy premises
- go slow - employees work at a slow rate
- work to rule - employees stick to their contracts absolutely; this often slows up their work considerably.
- strikes - employees refuse to work. To be official employees must have a secret ballot and gain a majority.

Determinants of union strength:

- the percentage of employees who are members (called the 'unionisation rate' or 'union density')
- the degree of public support
- management attitude
- legal environment
- the ability of management to find alternative labour
- union and management resources

Unions continued

Employment Laws

Major changes affecting unions include: 1980, 1982, 1988, 1989, 1990 Employment Acts, 1984 Trade Union Act, Trade Union Reform and Employment Rights Act 1993.

The effects of changes in the laws in the 1980s and 1990s include:

- a union must have a secret ballot before it can have an official strike

- a union is liable for damages if a strike is unofficial

- a code of practice recommends a maximum of 6 official pickets (employees who protest outside a factory to persuade others not to go to work)

- secondary picketing is illegal (i.e. workers can only protest at the place of work where the original dispute occurred; cannot try to influence employees at other places, e.g. suppliers or distributors)

- senior union officials must be elected at least every five years

- unions must provides at least seven days notice of official industrial action

Union membership has declined since the late 1970s. A major reason is the growth of employment in sectors where unions are not traditionally very strong, e.g. part timers, the service sector, south east, and women workers.

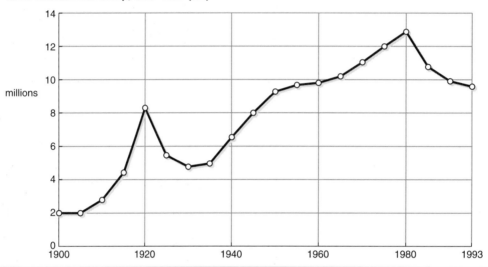

Trade union membership, 1900–1993 (UK)

Recent developments in industrial relations

- No strike agreements - trade unions agree not to strike in the case of a dispute; usually agree that if they cannot reach a solution the dispute will go to arbitration. Arbitration occurs when a third party decides to settle the dispute.

- Single union deals - management only recognise one union for the purpose of bargaining.

- Beauty contests - competition between trade unions to gain recognition by an employer, e.g. firm announces it will only bargain with one union so unions must compete for that right.

- Pendulum arbitration - a third party solves a dispute by choosing one side or the other; cannot compromise between the two sides; the idea is that this makes the two sides make more realistic claims in the first place.

Organisations

ACAS: Advisory Conciliation and Arbitration Service. Independent body set up by the Government in the 1970s. Provides advice to employers and employees on industrial relations. If asked it will attempt to bring the two sides in a dispute together (conciliate). If this does not work, ACAS (if asked by both sides) will solve the dispute by making the decision itself (arbitration).

TUC: Trades Union Congress. Represents most unions at national and international level; attempts to influence public opinion and Government.

CBI: Confederation of British Industry. Represents firms in private sector; attempts to influence public opinion and the government; attempts to promote image of industry; provides information on industry for members.

Employers' associations: represent employers' views and interests in a particular industry, e.g. EEF (Engineering Employees' Federation).

Motivation in theory

Motivation is the extent to which an individual makes an effort to do something

Key elements

NEEDS ↕ REWARDS

COMMUNICATION →

← PERCEPTION

To motivate:

- appropriate rewards must be offered
- individuals must know how to achieve these rewards
- individuals must believe they are capable of achieving them
- individuals must perceive the rewards are fair

Motivated employees are likely:

- to be more productive
- to have better attendance rates
- to be more co-operative and open to change
- to produce better quality work.

Theorists

Maslow's hierarchy of needs:

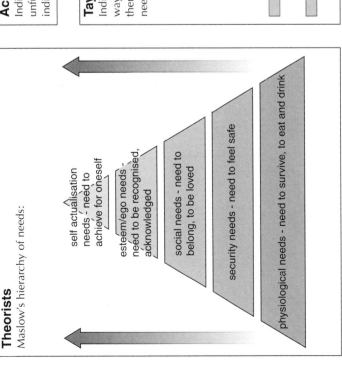

self actualisation needs - need to achieve for oneself

esteem/ego needs - need to be recognised, acknowledged

social needs - need to belong, to be loved

security needs - need to feel safe

physiological needs - need to survive, to eat and drink

According to Maslow:

Individuals will be motivated if the reward satisfies an unfulfilled need. Once satisfied a need no longer motivates; individuals will want the next level of need satisfied.

Taylor - Bethlehem Steel Works; Scientific Management. Individuals are motivated by money. Show them the best way to do a job so they can increase productivity. Reward them for higher output. This approach meets lower level needs.

security needs

physiological needs

Mayo - Hawthorne Works; Human Relations School. Individuals have social needs. They respond to being involved, working in teams, being listened to.

social needs

Herzberg's Two Factor Theory:

Hygiene factors: prevent dissatisfaction if they are present but do not actually satisfy e.g. acceptable working conditions, rules, basic pay

Motivators: factors at work which actually satisfy if they are present, e.g. responsibility, recognition, the chance of promotion

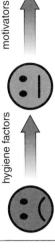 

hygiene factors

motivators

Vroom's Expectancy theory: The extent to which individuals believe that they can achieve the rewards which are offered affects their motivation. If they have a high expectancy (i.e are confident they can achieve the rewards) motivation is likely to be higher. If their expectancy that a reward can be achieved is low, they will be less motivated.

Equity theory: Rewards must be seen to be fair compared to what others get for their efforts.

Motivation in practice

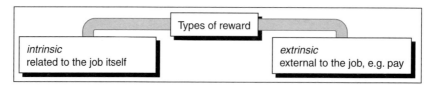

Types of reward

intrinsic	extrinsic
related to the job itself	external to the job, e.g. pay

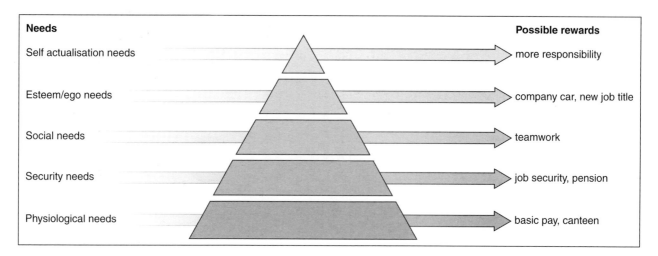

Needs

Self actualisation needs → more responsibility

Esteem/ego needs → company car, new job title

Social needs → teamwork

Security needs → job security, pension

Physiological needs → basic pay, canteen

Possible rewards

Motivating jobs should:
- provide variety
- allow individuals some responsibility
- provide employees with feedback
- provide employees with a complete unit of work, not just a small part of a job
- have a sense of purpose

Designing motivating jobs

- Job enrichment - employees are offered a more challenging job, with more responsibility. Called 'vertical loading'.

- Job enlargement - employees are offered more tasks to do; similar level of responsibility. Called 'horizontal loading'.

- Job rotation - individuals systematically moved from one job to another; provides variety and gives them a view of other areas of the firm.

- Autonomous work groups - teams set up and allowed to make their own decisions on, e.g. who does what. The team as a whole is held responsible for results.

- Delegation - subordinates entrusted with tasks by superiors. This frees management time and allows employees more responsibility.

- Multi skilling - training employees for a number of tasks.

- Empowerment - giving an employee power over their own work.

- Remove demarcation lines: demarcation lines define what one job consists of compared to another; this can act as a constraint by preventing employees undertaking other tasks. To increase flexibility management may attempt to negotiate the removal of demarcation lines

Reward systems

Payment systems:

- time - pay by the hour, e.g. shop assistants. Relies on individuals using their time productively.

- performance related pay - pay on performance, e.g. piece rate (employees paid for each unit of output). Should be motivating but quality can suffer as individuals rush to complete work. 'Commission' occurs when individuals are paid a percentage of sales. 'Measured day work' occurs when individuals agree a target output and are paid assuming this work is done. At the end of the period adjustment is made depending on actual output. BUT it can be difficult to measure output in some jobs, e.g. receptionist.

- salary - set amount per year; paid monthly. Shows that employers trust employees to use their time effectively.

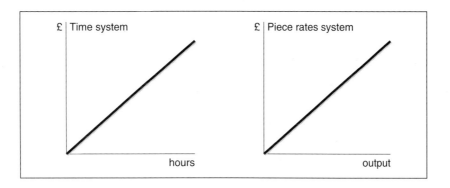

Incentive schemes:

- profit sharing - individuals receive a proportion of company profits

- bonus scheme - additional payments if set targets are exceeded

Fringe benefits:

- company car

- contributions to pension schemes

- contributions to health schemes

- subsidised canteen

- relocation allowance if moved an employee is from one area to another

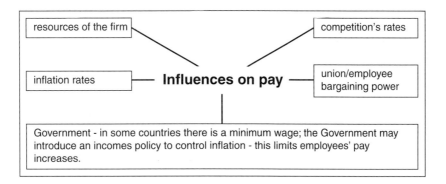

Successful reward systems
Successful reward systems will:

- attract and retain sufficient numbers of suitable employees

- reward employees for effort, experience, loyalty and achievement

Leadership

Leadership is the process of influencing others towards a shared goal.

Style theorists: believe that effective leadership depends on the way in which people are led, e.g autocratic or democratic.

Autocratic: leader tells employees

Democratic: leader discusses with employees and involves them in decisions

Laissez-faire: leader has little direct input; leaves subordinates to make decisions

Paternalistic: 'fatherly' style of leadership; employees treated as family members; leader tries to guide them; will tend to decide for them ('I know best')

Trait theories: believe that leadership depends on personal qualities (traits), e.g. a leader is naturally extrovert, charming, single minded. Studies have been unable to identify the same traits in all leaders, so the theory has limited practical use for firms.

The Tannenbaum Schmidt continuum: highlights the range of management style

Tells — leader presents final decision to subordinates

Sells — leader persuades subordinates why a decision has been made

Consults — leader asks for subordinates' opinions and then decides

Participates — leader involves subordinates and decision is made jointly

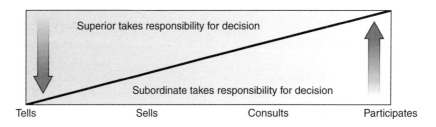

Superior takes responsibility for decision

Subordinate takes responsibility for decision

| Tells | Sells | Consults | Participates |

Blake Mouton's managerial grid: also shows a range of managerial styles

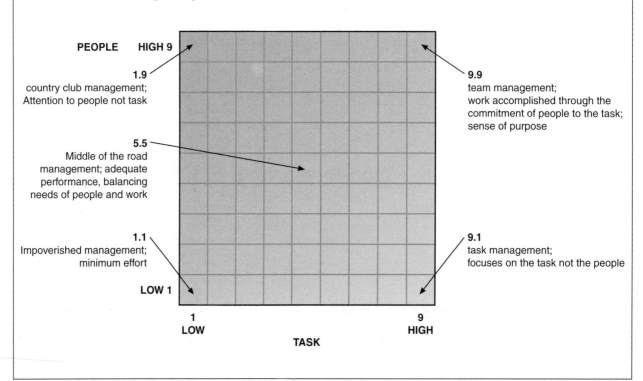

PEOPLE   HIGH 9

1.9
country club management;
Attention to people not task

9.9
team management;
work accomplished through the
commitment of people to the task;
sense of purpose

5.5
Middle of the road
management; adequate
performance, balancing
needs of people and work

1.1
Impoverished management;
minimum effort

9.1
task management;
focuses on the task not the people

LOW 1

1
LOW

9
HIGH

TASK

McGregor's Theory X and Theory Y: highlights the different assumptions which managers hold about employees.

Theory X managers seem to believe that employees:

are lazy

do not want to work

have to be controlled and monitored

↓

Theory X managers tend to be

↓

More autocratic

Theory Y managers seem to believe that employees:

want to work

want responsibility with appropriate rewards

↓

Theory Y managers tend to be

↓

More democratic - involve employees because they trust and value their input

---

Likert's model: again shows management styles

System 1: exploitative authoritative
power and direction from the top; threats and punishment used

System 2: benevolent authoritative; some opportunities for consultation

System 3: consultative; subordinates consulted; rewards rather than threats used

System 4: participative; subordinates fully involved in decisions

---

Situational approach: there is no one best way of leading - it depends on the situation and a number of variables.

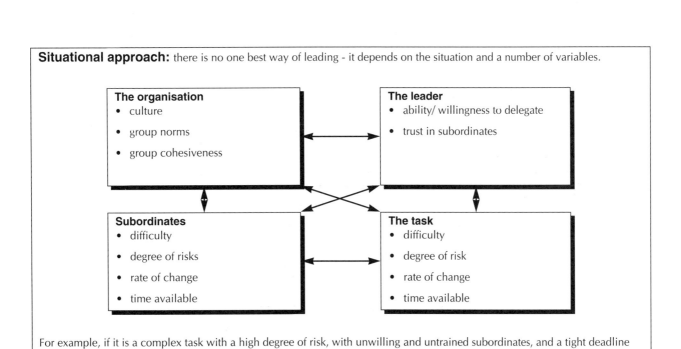

The organisation
- culture
- group norms
- group cohesiveness

The leader
- ability/ willingness to delegate
- trust in subordinates

Subordinates
- difficulty
- degree of risks
- rate of change
- time available

The task
- difficulty
- degree of risk
- rate of change
- time available

For example, if it is a complex task with a high degree of risk, with unwilling and untrained subordinates, and a tight deadline then an autocratic style is likely to be appropriate. If subordinates are willing and able, the manager is trusting, and the task is routine, a more democratic style might be the most successful.

Participation and involvement

Benefits of participation:
- more ideas
- gains employees' cooperation
- increases motivation
- less need for supervision
- better industrial relations

Methods of participation:
- Worker Directors - employee representative on the Board of Directors. Occurs in Germany and other continental countries but rare in UK.
- Works councils - employee representatives form a committee. Called a 'Betriebsrat' in Germany. They have a right to influence policies involving employees and appoint a director to the main board. Known as 'codetermination' because of employees right to codetermine (agree and formulate policy on) issues involving people. Some UK companies are setting up works councils, e.g. BT and ICI.
- Consultative committees - employee representatives are consulted on issues such as health and safety or new developments; deal with issues affecting the whole firm.
- Quality circles - voluntary group of employees, e.g. 5-12; meet during working hours to discuss problems relating to their work; present ideas to management.
- Team briefings - Manager meets with employees regularly to discuss issues relevant to their work. Objective is to make sure employees know and understand what they are doing and why.

Problems of participation:
- deciding which method
- costs
- time
- slower decision making
- limiting the extent
- interests may conflict

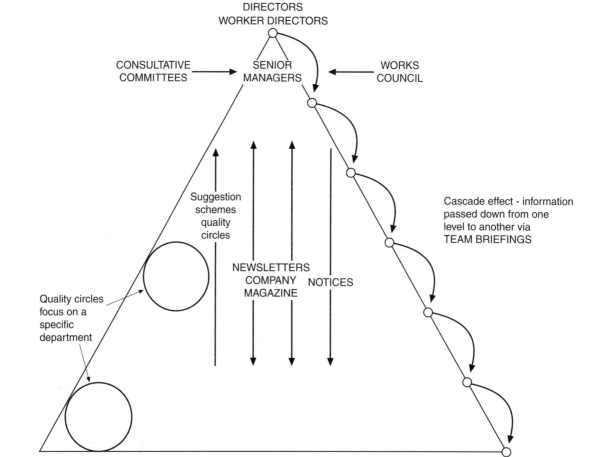

DIRECTORS
WORKER DIRECTORS

CONSULTATIVE COMMITTEES → SENIOR MANAGERS ← WORKS COUNCIL

Suggestion schemes quality circles

Cascade effect - information passed down from one level to another via TEAM BRIEFINGS

NEWSLETTERS COMPANY MAGAZINE   NOTICES

Quality circles focus on a specific department

Teams and groups

Firms are making increasing use of teams - groups of people with common goals and who are held mutually accountable for their actions.

Why use teams? Can delegate work to teams; develop individuals' skills and remove some of the need to supervise if the team monitors itself. Teams can meet individuals' social, esteem, and self actualisation needs. Teamwork can provide more flexibility and the ability to react to change quickly. Teams can share ideas and make use of each others' skills.

Good teamwork involves trust, support, cooperation, a sense of direction, listening, openness, individuals feeling able to express their ideas.

Good team members must have the technical skills required but also be able to work with others, e.g. be willing to listen and be flexible.

Types of groups:

formal - set up by the organisation, e.g. management teams

informal - set up by employees themselves, e.g. friends at work

Authority: legitimate power.

Responsibility: obligation to complete a task effectively.

Chain of command: line of command from top to bottom of organisation

Span of control: number of subordinates directly responsible to a superior. A narrow span enables managers to keep control and reduces risk. A wide span develops subordinates and enables them to have greater freedom; allows for less levels of management.

Size of span depends on: ability of subordinates to complete the task, whether the task is simple or complex; the ability of the superior to oversee employees; and the quality of communication.

Hierarchy: level of responsibility

Organisational chart: represents the organisational structure. It shows reporting relationships but does not show the authority of each position.

Formal organisation: deliberately planned authority relationships and communication channels.

Informal organisation: network of relationships and communication established by employees themselves. Not shown on an organisational chart.

Types of structure
- Tall, thin organisation, e.g. the army

This type of structure has a small span of control and many levels of hierarchy.

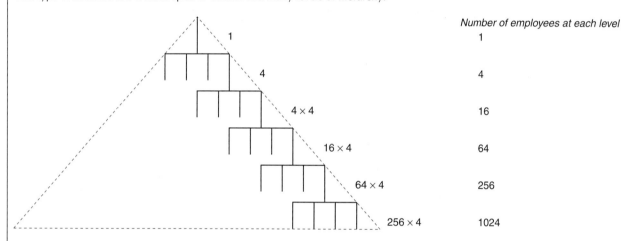

Number of employees at each level

1	1
4	4
4 × 4	16
16 × 4	64
64 × 4	256
256 × 4	1024

To oversee 1000 employees with a span of 4, 5 levels of hierarchy are needed.

- Wide, flat organisations, e.g. the church. This type of structure has wide spans of control but few layers of hierarchy. There are fewer chances of promotion but employees are likely to have more authority.

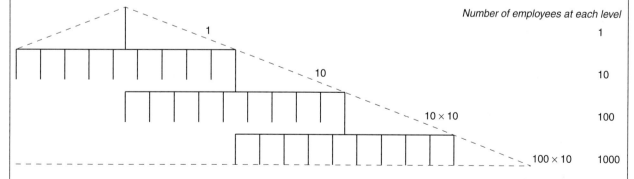

Number of employees at each level

1	1
10	10
10 × 10	100
100 × 10	1000

To oversee 1000 employees with a span of 10, 3 levels of hierarchy are needed.

A trend in the 1980s and 1990s is 'delayering' = less levels of hierarchy and wider spans; this increases the responsibility of employers and reduces the need for middle management.

Management structure continued

Departmentalisation: the grouping of jobs

By function:

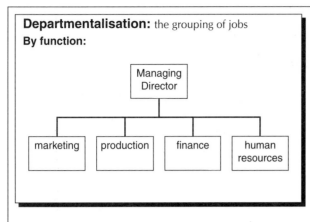

By region:

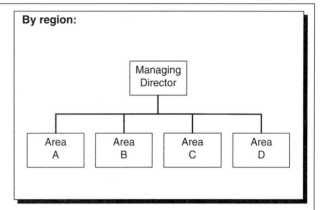

By product:

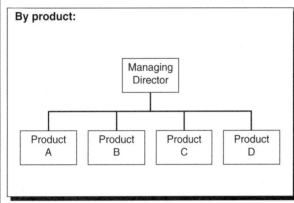

By type of customer:

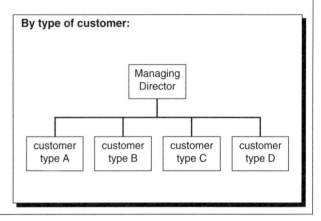

Matrix organisations: individuals have two or more superiors, e.g. if a project team is created, the marketing manager involved may be responsible to the project leader and to the marketing director.

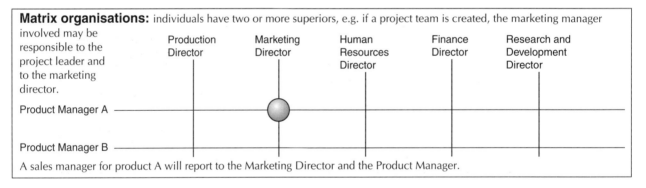

A sales manager for product A will report to the Marketing Director and the Product Manager.

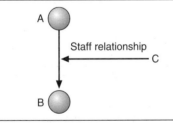

Line relationship: A to B; direct authority relationship, e.g. production manager to production supervisor

Staff relationship: C to A; advisory relationship which has no direct authority over the line; an expert or specialist who provides information to the line manager, e.g. market research or human resources function.

'Staff' sometimes get frustrated because they can only advise; line may not pay any attention.

Centralisation: main decisions made by senior management; little authority is passed down the organisation. Advantages: decisions made by experienced people with overview. Ensures policies are consistent throughout the organisation.

Decentralisation: extent to which authority passed down the organisation. Advantage: enables divisions or departments to react quickly to their market conditions.

The trend in the 1980s and 1990s is to decentralise to provide greater flexibility.

If the organisational structure is wrong:

- motivation may decrease - people do not know what is happening or why

- decision making can be slow

- lack of coordination

- costs can rise

- failure to share ideas

Political environment

The political environment concerns the role of the Government and its affect on organisations.

'Government' includes central and local government:

Central government

Departments include:

The Treasury- responsible for economic strategy

Departments: of Social Security (provides benefits), of Trade and Industry, of Transport

QUANGOs (specialised bodies with specific responsibilities, e.g. Sports Council and Arts Council)

Local authorities - include county councils and district councils. They provide services in their areas such as:

education and recreation, e.g. libraries and sports centres

housing, e.g. council houses

environmental services, e.g. refuse collection

road maintenance

social services, e.g. care for the elderly

Local authorities are funded by central government and the council tax.

The Government influences the economy through:

- Government spending - directly on goods and services, e.g. motorways and defence; indirectly through benefits, e.g. pensions

- Taxation - direct from earnings, e.g. income tax, corporation tax; indirectly placed on goods and services, e.g. VAT and excise duties

- Regional Policy - investment grants, low rents, loans available for specified areas where there are high levels of unemployment.

- Legislation, e.g. Competition Policy - to prevent unfair competition

The political environment includes the extent to which the Government intervenes in the economy.

Types of economy

Free market economy
resources are allocated by market forces of supply and demand

Mixed economy
mixture of free market and command economies; has private and public sector

Command or planned economy
Government allocates resources

The more interventionist a government is, the more it will regulate or interfere with the free market and move towards a command economy. A 'laissez-faire' approach to the economy means that the Government prefers to let the market mechanism work rather than intervene.

Private sector: organisations are controlled by private individuals, e.g. companies

Public sector: organisations are controlled by the Government, e.g. BBC

Political environment continued

Advantages of free market:
- incentive for producers as they keep the profits
- markets are responsive to consumer demand
- incentive to be efficient to keep costs down
- incentive to be innovative

Problems of command economy:
- lack of incentive as profits belong to the Government
- informational problems
- coordination problems if the Government tries to organise the whole economy.

The trend has been towards free market economies and less Government intervention, e.g privatisation and deregulation in Eastern Europe.

Problems of free market:
- inequality - can be large differences between rich and poor
- will not provide 'public goods', such as streetlighting; no one would pay for street lighting in a free market - individuals hope someone else will pay for them and that they will benefit anyway. They would try to be 'free riders'. The Government has to provide these goods.
- merit goods are underprovided. These are goods that individuals would not value sufficiently and so would not consume enough of them, e.g. healthcare, education
- instability - prices might fluctuate greatly in some markets, e.g. exchange rates; society might prefer stability
- resources may not reallocate efficiently, e.g if demand changes employees may be left unemployed
- 'external costs'- costs to society which the firm will not pay for in the free market, e.g. pollution; because firms would not account for these external costs they overproduce unless the Government intervenes. The total cost to society is the private costs to the firm + the external cost.

Privatisation involves the transfer of assets from public sector to the private sector.

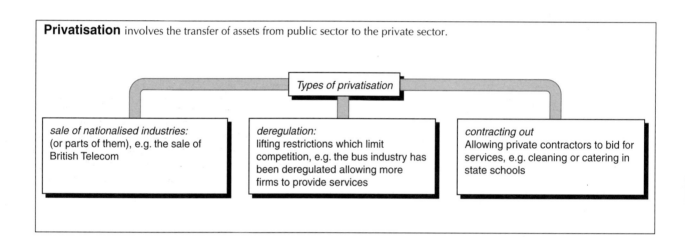

Types of privatisation

sale of nationalised industries:	deregulation:	contracting out
(or parts of them), e.g. the sale of British Telecom	lifting restrictions which limit competition, e.g. the bus industry has been deregulated allowing more firms to provide services	Allowing private contractors to bid for services, e.g. cleaning or catering in state schools

In the 1980s and 1990s the Conservative government privatised many industries,.e.g.

		Sold for:
1980 -1	British Steel	£509mn
1980-1	British Aerospace	£60mn
1980-1	National Freight Corporation	£100mn
1980-1	British Airways	£160mn
1989-90	Water companies	£5028mn
1994-5	British Coal	£1,633mn

Reasons for privatising:
- raises revenue for the Government
- creatse more competition
- frees organisations from political influence - decisions were sometimes made for political rather than business reasons
- increases share ownership

In the 1980s and early 1990s Government policy:
- privatised many industries
- focused on reducing inflation
- deregulated many businesses
- switched the emphasis from direct to indirect tax
- emphasised the role of the free market

Legal environment

Employment Law includes:

Sex Discrimination Act 1975: illegal to discriminate against someone because of their sex or marital status. Relates to, e.g. recruitment, terms and conditions, training, promotion, and dismissal.

Race Relations Act, 1976: illegal to discriminate against someone on the basis of race, ethnic group, colour.

Equal Pay Act, 1970: an employee doing the same or broadly similar work as a member of the opposite sex is entitled to equal rates of pay and conditions.

Equal Pay Act (Amendment) 1983: equal pay for work of equal value.

Redundancy Payments Act 1965: Employees who have worked continuously for an organisation for 5 year's part time or 2 years full time are entitled to notice and statutory redundancy pay (approximately 1 week for every year worked)

Health and safety:

Factories Act, 1961: Offices, Shops and Railway Premises Act 1963; these provide minimum requirements for safety.

Health and Safety at Work Act 1974: employers must ensure that as far as is reasonably practicable 'the health, safety and welfare of employees, covers, e.g. plant and working equipment, handling, storage and transportation of articles and substances, training and supervision

Enforced by Health and Safety Executive: can enter premises; can order improvements to be made.

Data Protection Act, 1984

to 'regulate the use of automatically processed information relating to an individual'

All users of personal data must register with the Registrar. Law states e.g. data should be adequate, relevant and not excessive; individuals are entitled to reasonable access; data should be accurate and up to date.

Competition Policy:

Responsibility of Office of Fair Trading which attempts to control anti competitive behaviour and protect consumers.

Legislation includes: 1948 Competition Act; 1973 Fair Trading Act.

Monopolies and Mergers Commission: recommends whether a monopoly or proposed merger is in the public interest. A monopoly exists if a firm has more than 25% of the market. Monopolies are referred to the MMC by the Office of Fair Trading; MMC can recommend that a merger is prohibited or, that firms end certain types of uncompetitive behaviour.

Restrictive trade practices: include price fixing and market sharing agreements. All restrictive practices have to be registered with the Office of Fair Trading. The Restrictive Practices Court decides whether to allow an agreement. It may be allowed if, e.g. it prevents local unemployment; operates against existing restrictions or maintains exports.

Consumer Law: includes

Weights and Measures Act, 1951: inspectors can test weighing and measuring equipment of organisations.

Trade Descriptions Act, 1968: prohibits false or misleading descriptions of goods or services

Sale of Goods Act, 1979: goods must be of merchantable quality (i.e. no serious flaws), fit for the purpose (i.e. can do what it is supposed to), and as described.

Supply of Goods and Services Act, 1982: these must be 'merchantable quality' and at 'reasonable rates'.

Consumer Protection Act, 1987: firms are liable for any damage which their defective goods might cause

Consumer Credit Act 1974: anyone offering credit must seek a licence from the Director General of Fair Trading and state the annual percentage rate charged (APR)

Contract Law: a contract is a legally binding agreement between two or more persons. If a contract is breached, the aggrieved party can seek damages or sue for 'specific performance'.

Tort: a tort is a 'civil wrong'; this includes a variety of activities such as negligence, e.g. if an employee is negligent; the employer can be liable as well (called vicarious liability).

Economic environment

National Income:

income in an economy is usually measured by:

GDP: Gross Domestic Product: value of final goods and services produced in an economy. This shows how much has been earned within a country.

or

GNP: Gross National product: value of final goods and services produced by factors of production owned by a country's residents. This shows how much has been earned anywhere in the world by a country's residents.

Trade Cycle

Over time the economy usually goes through booms and slumps. This is called the 'trade cycle' or business cycle.

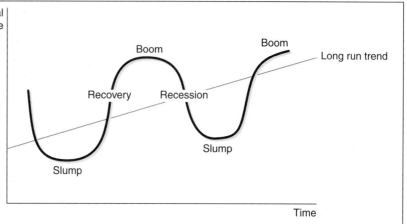

In a recession:

• demand for a firm's products may fall

• firms may have to cut back on overtime or make redundancies

• consumers may be more price sensitive

• stocks may increase and firms may have to decrease production

The effect of a recession depends on the size of the recession, the length of the recession, and the type of firm, e.g. food and pharmaceutical industries are fairly recession proof, whereas the housing, construction and car industries are sensitive to income changes. Shopping goods will be more sensitive than convenience goods to changes in the level of national income.

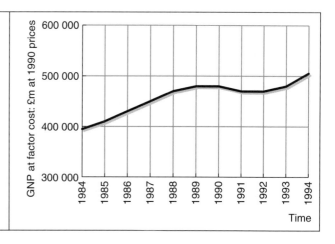

The objectives of Government include:

• growth   i.e. increase the income of the economy

• stable prices   i.e control inflation

• a healthy balance of payments   i.e. increase exports

• full employment   i.e. reduce unemployment

To achieve its objectives the Government uses:

monetary policy	*fiscal policy*	direct controls	direct intervention
• control of the money supply • changes in interest rates	• changes in taxation • changes in government spending	legislation, e.g. price controls	provision of certain goods, e.g. health care

exchange rate policy
increasing or decreasing the value of the currency

In many cases the government is trying to influence the total demand in the economy; this is called Aggregate Demand (AD)

Aggregate demand for a country's goods and services = consumers' spending (consumption C) + firms' spending (investment) + Government spending (G) + exports (X) - import spending (M)

$$AD = C + I + G + X - M$$

A reflationary policy increases aggregate demand, e.g. by cutting taxes, boosting spending or lowering interest rates. Aggregate Demand INCREASES.	A deflationary policy reduces aggregate demand, e.g. by increasing taxes, cutting spending or increasing interest rates. Aggregate Demand DECREASES.

Government spending: — % *of general Government expenditure*

Government spending:	1994
social security	34
health	14
education	13
defence	8
public order and safety	5
general public services	4
housing and community amenities	4
transport and communication	2
other	16
TOTAL in real terms	£285.7bn

Source : CSO

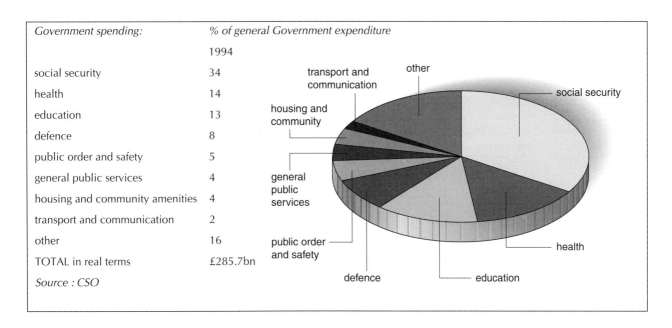

Taxes can be

indirect	placed on the goods or services themselves, e.g. VAT
direct	taken directly from income, e.g. income tax or corporation tax
progressive	take a higher proportion of income as income rises
regressive	take a smaller proportion of income as income rises
specific	certain amount (£) per unit
ad valorem tax	adds a given percentage to the price, e.g. VAT

Multiplier

The multiplier is based on the idea that one person's spending is another's income. If, for example, the government spends £10m to get a road built, this money will be earnt by construction companies, landowners and employees. These different groups will then spend some of their earnings buying other goods and services. Of the initial £10m, a proportion such as £8m will be spent on other products. The recipients of the £8m will also want to spend and so the initial injection by the government sets off a chain-reaction of spending. This is called the 'Multiplier effect'. If, for example, £10m is initially spent on goods and services this might eventually lead to a total of £50m worth of spending. In this case the multiplier is 5. The size of the multiplier depends on how much is spent at each stage in the chain - called the marginal propensity to consume (MPC). The higher the MPC, the more is spent at each stage and the higher the multiplier.

Budget position: financial position of the Government; Budget deficit - Government spending is greater than revenue; Budget surplus - Government revenue is greater than spending.

Public Sector Borrowing Requirement (PSBR): the amount of money the government has to borrow in a year to finance its deficit. Can be financed by selling IOUs (short term are called Treasury Bills, longer term are called bonds).

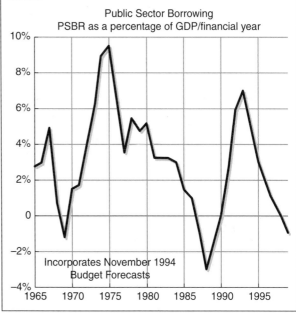

Supply side policies: aimed at improving the supply in the economy, e.g. reducing income tax to encourage people to work; reducing corporation tax to encourage firms to invest; increasing training; reducing benefits available for the unemployed to encourage people to work.

Interest rates and exchange rates

Interest rates: the cost of borrowing money and the reward offered to savers.

If interest rates increase:

- households are more likely to save and less likely to spend. This will affect income elastic goods more than income inelastic, e.g. the demand for shopping goods are likely to be more affected than the demand for convenience goods

- households discretionary income is likely to fall as more money is used to repay mortgages and loans (discretionary income = income after tax and regular bills)

- firms are likely to reduce their stocks because money tied up in stocks represents a greater opportunity cost

- debtors will want to hold onto their money to earn interest and are likely to delay payment

- creditors will want their money more quickly

- because of an increased desire to save in the UK the exchange rate might increase

---

Exchange rates

The exchange rate is the price of one currency in terms of another, e.g. it may cost 3 Deutschmarks to buy one pound.

In a free floating exchange rate system the value of the pound is determined by supply and demand for the currency. Demand for pounds (or sterling) is the demand to buy pounds with other currencies. The supply of pounds (or sterling) depends on the desire to change pounds into another currency.

If demand increases the price is likely to increase. If supply increases the price is likely to fall as more are available.

Demand for pounds may increase because of:

- more demand for UK goods and services

- greater desire to save in the UK

- more tourism to the UK

- speculators who believe that the pound will rise in the future so buy now

Supply of pounds may increase because of:

- greater demand for overseas goods and services

- greater desire to save abroad

- more tourism abroad

- speculators who believe that the pound will fall in the future so sell now

---

An increase in the pound is called an APPRECIATION; it means the pound is stronger.

A fall in the pound is called a DEPRECIATION; it means the pound is weaker.

£:$	1991	1992	1993	1994
	1.769	1.767	1.502	1.533

There are many exchange rates because the pound is exchanged for many other currencies, e.g. the yen, the deutschmark, the franc. It will have a price against each of these currencies.

Effective exchange rate: shows the value of a pound against a number of other currencies. It is calculated as a weighted index; each currency has a different weight according to its relative importance in trade with the UK.

A high or strong pound: means the pound is more expensive, i.e. it costs more in terms of foreign currency. This makes UK goods/services more expensive in foreign currencies but because a pound can be changed for more foreign currency it becomes cheaper to buy imports in pounds.

The effect of an increase in the pound:

- increases price of UK goods and services abroad; in terms of foreign currency; demand is likely to fall. The extent of the fall depends on how sensitive demand is to price (price elasticity of demand). However, some firms may decide not to increase price and accept lower profits
- imports become cheaper in pounds; may reduce input costs; may make it more difficult for domestic firms to compete against foreign competitors
- depends on how much pound has gone up and for how long
- depends which currencies it has increased against

Government and the exchange rate:

The Government can increase the value of the pound by:
- buying pounds with foreign currencies through the Bank of England
- increasing interest rates to make pounds more attractive to would be savers from abroad

In a fixed exchange rate system the government intervenes to keep the price constant or within a band.

Exchange Rate Mechanism (ERM): European currencies are fixed against each other but not against other currencies.

1990 UK joined ERM at a rate of 2.95 Dm (although it could move within a 6% band either way)
1992 UK left ERM - could not keep price fixed as it meant interest rates would have to be too high for the domestic economy.

ERM system

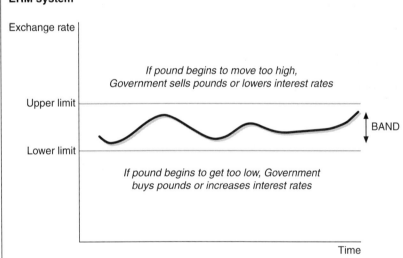

Inflation

Inflation is a persistent increase in the general price level. It is usually measured by the Retail Price Index (RPI).

The RPI measures the *cost of living*. It is a weighted index; the weights reflect the relative importance of goods to the average household.

RPI	1991	1992	1993	1994
	5.9	3.7	1.6	2.4

Source: British Economic Survey

Causes include:
- demand pull- too much demand for the number of goods. In this situation stocks are low and firms are able to increase their prices and profit margins, e.g. in the late 1980s the economy overheated as demand grew faster than supply.

- cost push - an increase in costs (e.g. wages or materials) forces producers to increase prices or accept lower profit margins, e.g in the mid to late 1970s prices increased due to sudden increases in oil prices which increased costs.

- monetary - excessive growth of the money supply - 'too much money chasing too few goods'. This is the Monetarist explanation of inflation.

Inflation:
- can lead to uncertainty which deters investment

- can lead to uncompetitiveness abroad (depending on what is happening to the exchange rate and prices overseas)

- can reduce purchasing power if unexpected or if individuals cannot gain pay increases to match inflation

- causes menu costs - the costs of changing, e.g. menus, brochures, slot machines

Wage price spiral: prices increase (e.g. due to too much demand), employees demand higher wages, this increases costs so prices increase and so on.

The effect of a firm increasing its prices depends on:
- what other firms are doing

- how sensitive demand is to price

- what is happening to income levels. If incomes are rising faster than prices the standard of living is actually increasing.

- what is happening to the exchange rate (if the firm exports).

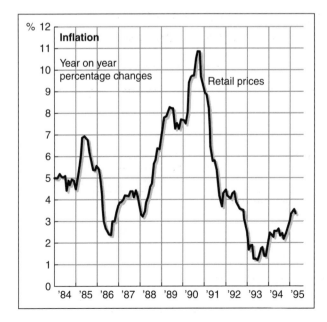

Controlling inflation:
- increase interest rates to deter spending

- restrict lending to deter spending

- increase exchange rate to make imports cheaper

- incomes policies - Government limits pay increases (this only tends to work in the short term as employees resist)

Unemployment

Unemployment:
Measured by the number of people claiming unemployment benefit.

annual average 000s	1991	1992	1993	1994
	2291.9	2778.6	2900.6	2620.8

Source: British Economic Survey

Unemployment rate: percentage of the working population which is unemployed.

Types of unemployment include:

- structural - people are unemployed because of the changing structure of the economy, e.g. a miner may not have the correct skills for the new jobs being created in computing.

- seasonal - people in jobs such as fruit picking are likely to be unemployed at certain times of the year.

- frictional - people between jobs, i.e. left one job and waiting before accepting another.

- residual - people who are unwilling to work or unable because of a disability

- cyclical - people are unemployed because of a lack of demand. Also called 'demand deficient' or Keynesian.

High unemployment may mean:

- less demand for goods and services

- a wider choice of labour for a firm

- a more co-operative workforce as employees are worried about their jobs

The effect of an increase in unemployment on a firm depends on:

- to what extent has unemployment increased?

- how long will the increase last for?

- in what areas has the unemployment occurred?

- what types of people are unemployed, e.g. what skills?

- is the firm aiming to expand?

International Trade

Based on comparative advantage; countries specialise in producing goods or services in which they have a comparative advantage, i.e. a lower opportunity costs,

e.g. if country A sacrifices 2X to make 1Y whereas country B sacrifices 3X, then A should specialise in producing Ys because it has the lower opportunity cost.

Free trade: no barriers to trade. The benefits should be wider choice for consumers and lower costs.

Free trade area: members remove barriers to trade amongst themselves, e.g. LAFTA - the Latin American Free Trade Area. Members can set their own tariffs with non members.

Customs Union: free trade amongst members and a common external tariff with non member countries, e.g. European Union.

Barriers to trade (protectionism):
- quotas - limit on quantity of goods allowed into a country
- tariffs - tax placed on imports
- technical barriers - regulations which make it difficult for foreign producers to sell their products
- exchange controls - limits on the amount of currency that can be changed into foreign currency to buy foreign goods.
- embargo - a ban on all trade in a particular good or service

Trade war: countries use protectionist measures against each other.

Countertrade: barter; countries/firms trade in goods rather than currencies

GATT: General Agreement on Tariffs and Trade - member countries aim to reduce barriers to trade

International competitiveness:
Depends on factors such as:
- price relative to competitors - the exchange rate can have a major influence
- quality of product (i.e. to what extent does it meet customer needs?)
- reliability of the product
- overall service, e.g. delivery times

Why protect?
- save jobs in particular industries
- give small firms time to grow and improve (infant industries)
- to maintain a way of life (e.g. farming)
- to keep control of strategically important industries, e.g. defence industries
- retaliation

Balance of payments: revenue generated from exports sold abroad v spending on imports. Balance of payments surplus - more is spent on a country's exports than it spends on imports. Balance of payments deficit - country spends more on imports than it receives from exports.

Balance of payments

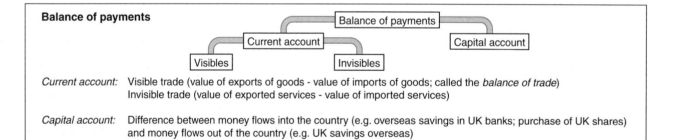

Current account: Visible trade (value of exports of goods - value of imports of goods; called the *balance of trade*)
Invisible trade (value of exported services - value of imported services)

Capital account: Difference between money flows into the country (e.g. overseas savings in UK banks; purchase of UK shares) and money flows out of the country (e.g. UK savings overseas)

Balance of payments of the UK (£m)

	1990	1991	1992	1993	1994	1995
Visible balance	−18809	−10284	−13104	−13378	−10831	−11550
Invisible balance	−484	1751	3636	2336	8751	4880
Current balance	−19293	−8533	−9468	−11042	−2080	−6670

Source: CSO

Import penetration: sales of foreign goods as a percentage of the total sales of a market.

Europe

Membership
In 1996 there were 15 members of the European Union: Belgium, France, Germany, Italy, Luxembourg, the Netherlands, Denmark, Iceland, the UK, Greece, Portugal, Spain, Austria, Finland and Sweden. A number of other countries in central and eastern Europe have applied for membership and are likely to join in the near future (e.g. Turkey, Poland, Hungary, Romania).

European Monetary Union
All members of the European Union (except the UK) have agreed to monetary union. This should lead to a single currency in Europe.

Key dates:
1957	European Economic Community set up.
1973	UK joined European Union
1986	Single European Act; aimed to create 'an area without internal frontiers in which the free movement of goods, persons, services and capital is ensured.'
1990	UK joins Exchange Rate Mechanism
1991	Maastricht Treaty
1992	UK leaves Exchange Rate Mechanism

The European Economic Community was set up to create a free trade area in which member states would trade without quotas and tariffs. By 1986 it was obvious that some barriers still existed, e.g. differences in regulations made it difficult to transport goods from one country to another. The aim of the Single European Act was to create an area in which there was freedom of movement of goods, services, labours and capital. Member countries were given until 1992 to bring this about. The result was a harmonisation of regulations.

European Union institutions:
The Council: the European Union's decision making body. It agrees legislation based on proposals from the Commission. There are, in fact, several councils (e.g foreign affairs, agriculture, finance); attended by the relevant ministers from member states and by the Commission.

The Commission:
- proposes community policy and legislation
- implements decisions taken by the Council of Ministers

Consists of commissioners appointed by the Community governments.

The European Parliament: directly elected every five years. Consulted on proposals for EC law. Can influence shape of laws and has power of veto in certain areas.

The European Union provides UK firms with:
- bigger markets; potential for growth and economies of scale
- more market opportunities
- more sources of employees
- greater competition
- more sources of finance
- incentive and opportunity to become efficient and learn from other firms
- the same safety and technical standards for many products
- the ability to compete for contracts from member governments
- the removal of border controls and lower administration costs.

In 1995 the EU took 58% of the UKs exports compared with 36% in 1973

Social Chapter (part of Maastricht treaty): proposals for employees concerning conditions, participation, working hours, protection of children, disabled persons, collective bargaining. The UK has not agreed to the Social Chapter.

Common Agricultural Policy: scheme to maintain the price of foodstuffs in Europe. If too much is produced the European Union buys up the excess to prevent the price falling below a set level. In practice the intervention price has been set too high so that the Union is regularly buying up food to stop the price falling. This has led to large stocks building up, e.g. wine lakes and butter mountains.

Social environment and technology

> **The social environment:** includes the values, attitudes, needs and expectations of consumers, employees, the Government, pressure groups, and investors. The social environment also includes demographic factors, such as the size of the population and its age structure.

Recent social trends in the UK include:

- growing environmentalism
- growing interest in health and fitness
- growing concern about the ethics of organisations
- more leisure time
- earlier retirement
- more women in the workforce

- increasing living standards
- slow population growth in UK
- decline in availability of younger workers
- ageing population
- more skilled and educated workforce
- more temporary and part time employment

The effect of changing social trends depends on:

- the type of firm, e.g. Mothercare will be affected by birth rates; retirement homes will be affected by the ageing population
- the size of trend and how long it lasts, e.g. will consumers still be concerned about ethics if the economy goes into a recession?

Statistics

The UK population is increasing at a slow rate:

Year	Population (000s)
1984	56506
1985	56685
1986	56852
1987	57009
1988	57158
1989	57358
1990	57561
1991	57808
1992	58006
1993	58191
1994	58395

Source CSO Office of Population Censuses and Surveys

Age structure of the UK (1991):

	%
under 16	20.3
16–39	35.2
40–64	28.7
65–79	12.0
80+	3.7
	100

Source: Social Trends

- Ethnic minorities form around 5% of the UKs population
- Over 25% of all households in the UK are people living alone

Technology

Technology is the way in which work is done, i.e. the equipment used and the way work is organised.

Improvements in technology lead to new products and processes.

The effects of technology include:
- new ways of working, e.g. more people working from home
- greater productivity/efficiency
- new products and markets, e.g. videocameras, microwaves
- more flexible manufacturing e.g computer aided design
- new skills needed

- loss of some jobs/creation of others
- improved communication, e.g. faxes, mobile phones
- shorter product life cycles
- quicker development times

When adopting technology firms should consider:
- initial cost
- employees' reaction
- training required
- expected benefits.

Social responsibility

An organisation may feel responsible to:

- employees, e.g. to provide motivating jobs, to provide job security
- the community, e.g. to protect the environment, to employ local people
- suppliers, e.g. to pay on time
- customers, e.g. to keep informed, to provide value for money

Pressure groups:

Organisations formed by people with a shared interest, which seek to influence public opinion and Government policy.

Interest groups: established to serve the interests of members, e.g. trade unions

Cause groups: established to promote a cause, e.g. environmentalist groups such as Greenpeace, Friends of the Earth

Other examples of pressure groups:

Institute of Directors: employers' pressure group; lobbies Government

Institute of Management: professional association of managers

Employer's Associations: employers' organisations for employers in the same industry.

Pressure group activities include:

- boycotting products, e.g. do not buy animal fur products
- media campaign, e.g. 1996 Greenpeace pressurised Shell into not dumping the Brent Spar oil rig in the sea
- lobbying government, i.e. putting views across, e.g. the brewers lobbied Government to change its legislation on ownership of pubs in the 1980s
- demonstrations and petitions

Environmental issues include:

- waste minimisation
- recycling
- energy efficiency
- protecting the ozone layer
- environmental labelling

BS7750: certificate which is awarded to firms achieving acceptable environmental standards.

Social audit: assessment of the effect of the firm's activities on society, e.g. amount of pollution, waste

Insider pressure groups: are regularly consulted by the Government, e.g. British Medical Association.

Outsider groups: do not have such easy access to the Government.

Effectiveness of pressure groups depends on:
- number of members
- resources
- public support
- ability to influence media and politicians

Ethics: a view about what is right and wrong, what is moral

Ethical issues include:
- should firms use child labour?
- what wages should firms pay in the Third World?
- to what extent should firms seek to be environmentally friendly?
- should firms get involved in certain activities, e.g. making weapons?

Why should organisations behave ethically?
- because their owners want them to
- to attract ethical investors, e.g. the CoOp Bank
- to attract ethical consumers
- to attract employees
- to avoid unfavourable media attention

Why should firms not behave ethically?
- they do not have to provided they behave legally
- it can impose extra costs
- there is no agreement on what is ethical
- can be conflict of interests, e.g. by not producing cigarettes they may have to make employees redundant

Change

Change is the one constant: there are always new markets, new products, new processes, new values and attitudes and developments in technology. Some firms embrace change - others resist it.

Internal change includes: employees' motives, behaviour, skills, product design

External change includes: PEST factors - political, economic, social, and technological

Resistance to change occurs because individuals:
- may not see the point
- prefer the existing arrangements - change may involve extra efforts, may lose status
- are afraid that they will not be able to perform as well in new situation; uncertain
- do not think that the proposed change is appropriate

Reaction to change can include: fear, resentment, anxiety, frustration, and anger.

Managing change:
- plan carefully
- explain need and purpose of it
- show benefits of it
- involve employees in it
- pay attention to speed of change
- train
- negotiate
- if necessary, coerce and force change through

Culture:
The attitudes, beliefs and values of the employees of an organisation. Influences how the employees think and act. Some organisations are entrepreneurial and innovative - employees encouraged to take initiative, e.g. 3M; others are bureaucratic - employees encouraged to stick to the rules. When organisations merge or there is a takeover, there can be a culture clash as they do things in different ways.

Types of culture (based on Harrison's model):
- power - relies heavily on the senior managers who retain control over all major decisions; often found in a company managed by the owners
- role- emphasis is on the position of individuals in the hierarchy; individuals have power through their position
- task - emphasis is on 'getting the job done'; individuals have authority through their ability to contribute to the task, e.g. through their expert knowledge
- person - emphasis is on the people within the organisation and their relationships; rare

Communication

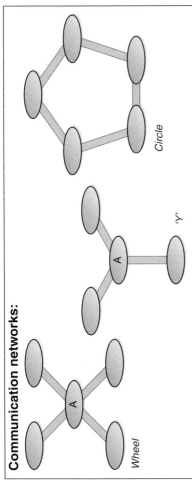

Types of communication

Vertical: up and down the organisation; downward is from superiors to subordinates e.g. giving orders, setting targets; upward is employee to employer, e.g. presenting a report

Lateral: communication across the organisation, e.g. one team member to another

Verbal: using words (whether they are spoken or written down)

Non verbal: not using words, e.g. body language

Formal: using the channels of communication established by the organisation.

Informal: using channels established by the employees themselves. Often called the grapevine. Passes information around quickly but information is often distorted

One way: sender does not receive feedback, e.g. manager puts up notice on noticeboard

Two way: sender receives feedback, e.g. manager discusses an issue with an employee at a meeting.

Slower than one way but sender gains more information

Communication networks:

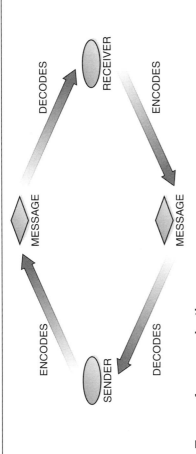

Wheel

'Y'

Circle

Used to examine the effect of information flowing in different ways between people.

Networks such as the wheel and the 'Y' are centralised: information must pass through a central position (labelled A). The circle is decentralised - information passes around. For complex problems decentralised networks tend to produce a quicker solution, fewer mistakes, and a more satisfied group. (In centralised networks A becomes overloaded and members do not all have effective input).

For simpler problems a centralised structure is quicker and makes fewer errors.

Barriers to communication:

Jargon -   words or phrases not known to the receiver

Noise -   any form of interference which makes it difficult to receive, e.g. actual noise or use of complicated words

Emotional state - if the receiver is upset, angry or depressed he or she can misinterpret

Distrust -   if employees do not trust their employer, this affects their interpretation of the message

Suitability of the channel - e.g. a long list of sales figures might be easier to understand if written down.

Location -   e.g. communication is more difficult if parts of the business are on different sites.

Results of poor communication:

- low morale
- high level of errors
- hostile relations
- lack of control

Information technology

> **Information technology:** the collection, storage, processing, and communication of information by electronic means.
>
> Enables large quantities of information to be handled quickly and economically.

Benefits of information technology:
- quicker handling of data
- better decision making because of easier access to information
- ability to consider 'what if'? scenarios easily
- increased productivity
- less waste

What is 'good' information?
- reliable
- accurate
- intelligible
- up to date
- complete
- appropriate level of detail
- available in a useful format
- cost effective

Information as a resource:
- essential for planning, organising, motivating, and controlling
- can provide a competitive advantage
- can improve performance and productivity

Problems with information technology:
- cost of selection, installation, maintenance
- training and retraining

Uses of information technology:

Data management:
enables more effective maintenance, updating, and manipulation of data, e.g. keeping of personnel and financial records

Communication:
enables easier communication between people, e.g. fax machines, mobile phones

Manufacturing:
used in systems such as computer integrated manufacture, can improve areas such as quality control, materials handling and stock control

Decision support:
enables better decisions by collecting, analysing and manipulating data more effectively

Office automation:
more effective performance with increased use of spreadsheets, word processors, desktop publishers, and telecommunications links such as electronic mail.

Management information systems:
provide information for planning and control, e.g. sales figures

Expert systems: cover a particular area of expertise and draw conclusions from computer stored knowledge obtained from specialists. Their purpose is to capture the expertise of key people and make their knowledge available to users of the programme, e.g. used to diagnose patients' symptoms

Database: set of files organised to enable easy access, e.g. personnel or customer records.

Spreadsheets: allow managers to set up mathematical models and investigate effects of different strategies, i.e. analyse 'what if'? questions.

Fax: technique for transmitting text and black and white pictures over the telephone network.

Electronic mail: way of sending text messages via a computer network.

EDI: electronic data interchange between organisations

EPOS: electronic point of sale e.g. scanning equipment at supermarket check-outs

CD ROM: compact discs for read only data storage

Bar code: a code in the form of parallel lines of varying widths which is used to enter data into computer via a scanner.

video conferencing: method of holding conferences via telecommunications network; individuals can see and hear each other.

Presenting and analysing data

- **Pie chart:** the proportion of the area of the circle shows the relative importance of items.

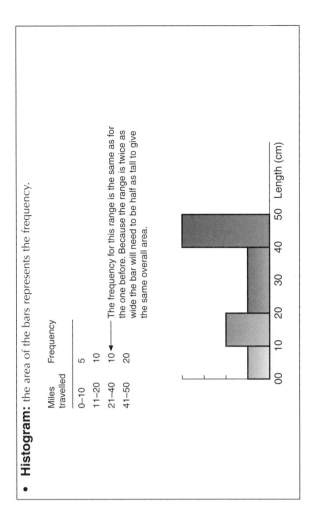

Product	Sales £m	% of total	Angle of segment (% of 360°)
A	50	16.6	60
B	100	33.3	120
C	150	50	180
	300		360°

Problems: difficult to illustrate more than a few items; cannot easily calculate the exact value of each item from looking at the diagram.

- **Histogram:** the area of the bars represents the frequency.

Miles travelled	Frequency
0–10	5
11–20	10
21–40	10
41–50	20

→ The frequency for this range is the same as for the one before. Because the range is twice as wide the bar will need to be half as tall to give the same overall area.

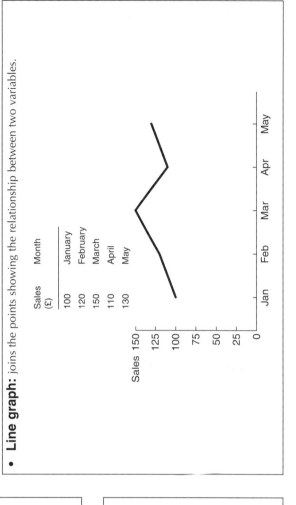

- **Pictogram:** Data is presented pictorially; eyecatching means of displaying data.

Problem: not easy to show figures accurately, e.g. if each person above represents 1000 employees – how do we show 246 employees?

- **Line graph:** joins the points showing the relationship between two variables.

Month	Sales (£)
January	100
February	120
March	150
April	110
May	130

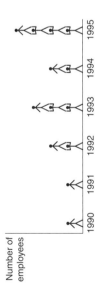

- **Bar chart:** length of bar shows the value of different items.

Product	Sales £ sales
A	50
B	100
C	150

Presenting and analysing data continued

Index numbers: these show how much an item has changed relative to a given starting point (called the base). The base is usually expressed as 100 so the index shows the percentage change compared to the base.

	X	
1991	100	
1992	120	X has increased by 20% since 1991
1993	90	X has fallen by 10% since 1991
1994	130	X has increased by 30% since 1991

Measures of central tendency:

Data: 2,12, 4, 14, 5, 6, 5, 7,10

mean - average; take the sum of the items and divide by the number of items. Total = 65. Number of items = 9. Mean = 65 ÷ 9 = 7.2.

median - middle value; rank items from the lowest to highest; choose middle value.
2, 4, 5, 5, 6, 7, 10, 12, 14. Middle value = 6.

mode - most frequent value; in this case 5

Normal distribution:
Statistical model; used with large samples (e.g. in marketing research and quality control) to help firms assess the likely results for the 'population' as a whole.

Features:
- Continuous, symmetrical, bell shaped distribution (i.e. most values cluster around the mean but there are some which are much higher or lower e.g. in a test the majority of students will get around the average score but a few will do much better or worse)
- The mean, mode, and median are equal
- 50% of the values lie either side of the mean

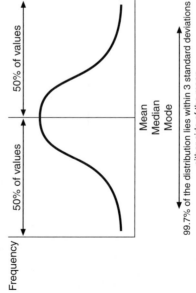

Frequency

50% of values   50% of values

Mean
Median
Mode

99.7% of the distribution lies within 3 standard deviations either side of the mean

95% of the distribution lies within 1.96 standard deviations either side of the mean

68% of the distribution lies within 1 standard deviation either side of the mean
(*Standard deviation* is a measure of how data is distributed around a mean value.)

Calculation:

z value = $(x - m) \div s$ where $x - m$ is the deviation from the mean and s = standard deviation. It shows how many standard deviations 'x' is from the mean.

Example. Mean weight of product is 500grams; standard deviation is 20

Question: what proportion of the products will be over 520 grams?

$z = 520 - 500 \div 20 = 1$ standard deviation from the mean. The area under the normal curve shown by this value can be read from tables. In this case it is 0.3413.

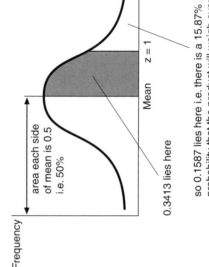

Frequency

area each side
of mean is 0.5
i.e. 50%

0.3413 lies here

Mean $z = 1$

so 0.1587 lies here i.e. there is a 15.87% probability that the product will weigh over 520

Limitations of the normal distribution: need a large sample size to get a normal distribution. Even then not all distributions will be normal.

Methods of smoothing data:

a. Moving average -

The trend line is smoother than actual sales figures; it eliminates fluctuations and highlights the trend more clearly.

year	sales		3 year moving average
1990	10		
1991	11	$\frac{10+11+12}{3}$	= 11
1992	12	$\frac{11+12+19}{3}$	= 14
1993	19	$\frac{12+19+11}{3}$	= 14
1994	11	$\frac{19+11+18}{3}$	= 16
1995	18		

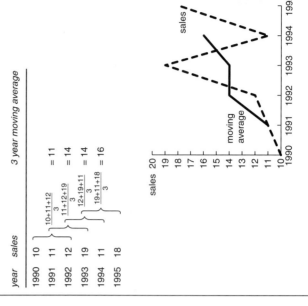

b. exponential smoothing - gives more emphasis to more recent data by giving it more weight when calculating the trend.

Forecasting

Forecasting: used to predict what might happen, e.g. what sales might be next year.

---

1 Time series analysis: based on extrapolation, i.e. projecting a past trend into the future. Assumes the past is an indicator to the future.

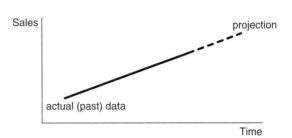

When using past data, firms will often 'smooth' the data to identify the underlying trend (look at page 86).

---

2 Causal modelling: tries to explain the causes of the data. Attempts to link one set of data with another, e.g. advertising and sales. Correlation measures the strength and direction of the link.

Correlation coefficients range from:

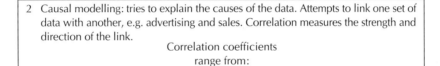

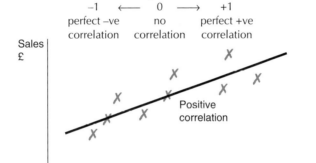

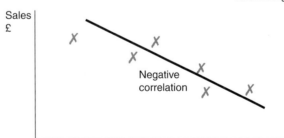

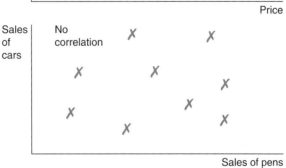

---

3 **Qualitative forecasts:** based on personal judgement or experts' opinions, e.g. use Delphi technique - experts asked independently for their views; responses collated and presented back to them; further comments accepted and incorporated. As experts comment independently, no one expert can dominate.

Operations research

Operations research: scientific approach to decision making; uses mathematical models;

Linear programming: sets out problems as a series of linear (straight line) equations.

Linear programming includes *Blending*: this shows how a firm can best allocate its resources given various constraints, such as allocating production between two products.

Example:
Minutes taken on different operations to produce two products:

	Operation 1	Operation 2
Product A	4 minutes	2 minutes
Product B	2 minutes	5 minutes
Total time available	*800 minutes*	*1200 minutes*

Constraints:

- Operation 1 4A + 2B ≤ 800, i.e it takes 4 minutes to make one A and 2 minutes to make a B and the maximum time available is 800 minutes. If all this time is spent on A then 200As are produced (800 ÷ 4). If all the time is spent on B, 400Bs can be produced. (See diagram I)

- Operation 2 2A + 5B ≤ 1200. If all the time was spent on A, 600 can be produced (=1200 ÷ 2). If all the time is spent on B, 240 can be made (=1200 ÷ 5). See diagram II.

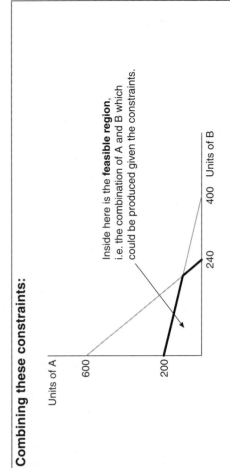

Diagram I

Line shows maximum of A and B which can be produced in Operation 1 given the time constraints

Units of A 200

Units of B 400

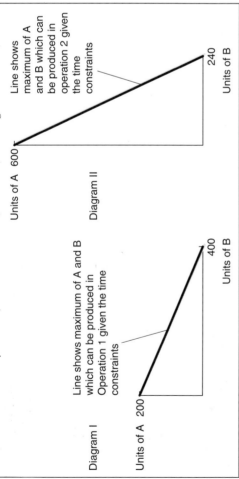

Diagram II

Line shows maximum of A and B which can be produced in operation 2 given the time constraints

Units of A 600

Units of B 240

Combining these constraints:

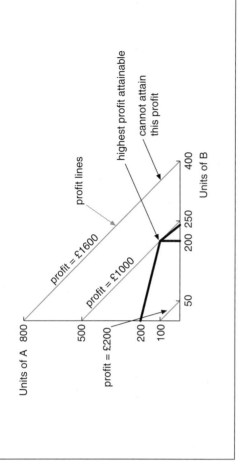

Units of A

600

200

240   400   Units of B

Inside here is the **feasible region**, i.e. the combination of A and B which could be produced given the constraints.

To maximise profits a firm must consider the profit per product, e.g. £2 for each A and £4 for each B.

To make a profit of £200 the firm could sell 100 As or 50 Bs

To make a profit of £400 the firm could sell 200As or 100Bs

To make a profit of £1000 the firm could sell 500As or 250Bs

The firm draws profit lines for each level of profit and sees the highest profit attainable given the constraints available.

Units of A 800

500

200

100

profit = £1600

profit = £1000

profit = £200

profit lines

highest profit attainable

cannot attain this profit

50   200 250   400   Units of B

Network analysis

Network analysis: used to estimate the minimum time to complete an operation and anticipate which tasks might cause bottlenecks. It helps encourage planning and enables materials to be purchased Just in Time.

Arrows: represent activities and often have a letter next to them to identify them; the length of time the activity takes (its duration) is put underneath the arrow.

Circles: (or nodes) represent the start or end of an activity.

A node has three sections: the left hand side shows a node number to make it easier to follow the order of tasks;

The top right shows the Earliest Start Time (EST) which is the earliest time the next task can begin.

Bottom right shows the Latest Finishing Time (LFT) which is latest time the previous task can finish without delaying the next task.

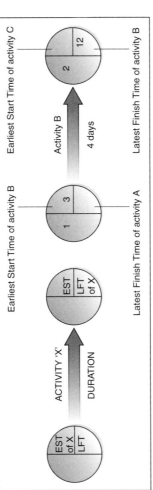

Total Float: this is the maximum increase in the time taken for an activity without increasing the overall time needed for the project; given by the Latest Finish Time - duration-Earliest Start Time, e.g. if an activity takes 4 days, has to finish on day 12 but can begin on day 3 then its total float is 12 - 4 - 3 = 5 days.

Free Float: maximum increase in time taken for this activity that can occur without altering the floats available to other activities. Free float = EST at end - duration - EST at start

Critical path: the sequence of events which determines the minimum time required to complete the project.

Critical path activities have no float. They must be started as soon as the previous ones finish. Non-critical activities have float time.

Transportation

Transportation: used to solve problems of transporting items from a number of different places to different destinations.

Example

Factory A Output	: 10	
Factory B Output	: 14	
TOTAL	: 24	

Warehouse 1 Capacity	: 12	
Warehouse 2 Capacity	: 10	
Warehouse 3 Capacity	: 2	
TOTAL	: 24	

The costs of transporting from each factory to each warehouse are as below:

£ per unit	Warehouse 1	Warehouse 2	Warehouse 3
Factory A	4	2	3
Factory B	1	5	1

Question: What is the most cost effective means of transporting materials from the factories to the warehouses?

To answer: construct a matrix and try different options. In the matrix below all of factory A's output is sent to Warehouse 1, so none is sent to the other two factories. The output of Factory B is then divided between the three factories according to their capacity.

these boxes show the cost of transporting from one warehouse to one factory

	Warehouse 1		Warehouse 2		Warehouse 3		Total
Factory A	10	4	0	2	0	3	10
Factory B	2	1	10	5	2	1	14
Total	12		10		2		24

Total cost = $(10 \times £4) + (2 \times £1) + (10 \times £5) + (2 \times £1) = £94$

Other options must then be tried to see if there are cheaper means of organising the deliveries; the cheapest method is called the 'least cost' solution, e.g. the option below gives a total cost of $(12 \times £1) + (10 \times £2) + (2 \times £1) = £34$

	Warehouse 1		Warehouse 2		Warehouse 3		Total
Factory A	10	4	0	2	0	3	10
Factory B	2	1	10	5	2	1	14
Total	12		10		2		24

Operations research continued

Activity	Duration	
A	2	must be done first
B	3	can only start after A is completed
C	4	can only start after A is completed
D	5	can only start when B is completed
E	8	can only start when C is completed
F	3	can only start when E is completed
G	4	can only start when D and F are completed

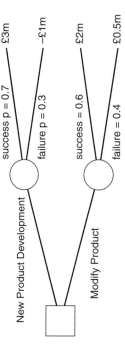

In days	EST	LFT	Duration	FLOAT	FREE FLOAT
A	0	0	2	0	0
B	2	12	3	7	0
C	2	6	4	0	0
D	5	17	5	7	7
E	6	14	8	0	0
F	14	17	3	0	0
G	17	21	4	0	0

Dummy activity: links interdependent events even though no time or resources are consumed by the link

e.g. D must follow A and B
C must follow A only

PERT analysis: programme evaluation and review techniques. Takes into account the fact that the duration of activities is uncertain. Instead of a single estimate of each activity time, it uses three estimates - most likely, optimistic (shortest estimate), pessimistic (longest estimate). Often used when delays possible, e.g. weather affecting construction

---

Decision trees: method of tracing alternative outcomes of decisions and comparing forecasted results.

Aid to decision making; aim is to reduce risk.

Squares are called 'decision nodes': these are points where decisions have to be made - the decision maker has to choose between different courses of action, e.g. to invest in a new advertising campaign or to develop new product.

Circles are called 'chance nodes' or 'event nodes'; they represent a point where there is a chance event. At an event node it is shown that a particular course of action can lead to several outcomes, e.g. success or failure.

The likelihood of a particular outcome is shown by the probability. If it is absolutely certain the probability is 1; if there is no chance of it happening the probability is 0; the more probable it is the closer the value will be to 1.

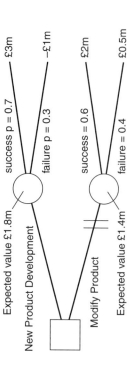

The expected value of each outcome = the predicted profit/loss x the probability of it occurring, e.g. the expected value of the new product development succeeding = 0.7 x £3m = £2.1m

The expected value of a particular course of action = the sum of the expected values of the possible outcomes, e.g. the expected value of new product development = expected value of success + expected value of failure = (0.7 x £3m) + (0.3 x -£1m) = £1.8m

Expected value of modifying product = (0.6 x £2m) + (0.4 x £0.5m) = £1.4m

The decision maker considers the expected value of each course of action and chooses the most profitable.

The option which is not selected is usually crossed off with two small lines.

Choose new product development because it has the highest expected value.

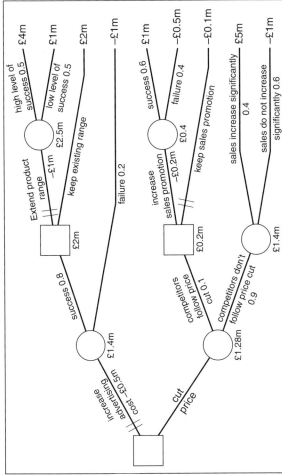

Operations research continued

Decision trees: help logical thinking, and, by constructing the tree, managers sometimes think of new courses of action; it makes managers think in terms of financial outcomes; it forces manager to think about risks and probability.

BUT the usefulness of a decision tree will depend on the underlying data - if the figures are incorrect, the technique is limited. Also they take time to construct and they show the situation at a particular moment in time, i.e. they are static; by the time the decision is made they may not be relevant. Another limitation is that they do not take into account non numerate information.

Simulation: (= queueing theory) involves constructing a model to simulate the effect of random events, e.g. customers appearing in shops and taking different lengths of time to serve. It deals with problems such as congestion at airports and queues in banks and aims to plan events so a bottleneck does not occur.

Example

time between arrivals (minutes)	frequency of customers %	cumulative frequency %
0	5	5
1	10	15
2	55	70
3	30	100

time at check-out (minutes)	frequency of customers %	cumulative frequency %
1	22	22
2	20	42
3	38	80
4	20	100

Random number table:

14→ 44 →73 →87
46　70　53　2
29　81　57　94
39　98　74　22
56　16　80　10

The random numbers are allocated to 'time between arrivals' and 'time at checkout' according to the cumulative frequencies as shown below in columns 3 and 6. Random numbers are then selected for each customer. If the random number picked out for the first customer to arrive is 14, this lies in the cumulative frequency range of 06-15 and so a time of 1 minute is allotted. If the random number selected for the time spent at the check-out is 44 this is in the range 43-80 so a time of 3 minutes is alloted.

time between arrivals	cumulative frequency	random numbers
0	5 →	01-05
1	15 →	06-15
2	70 →	16-70
3	100 →	71-100

time at check out	cumulative frequency	random numbers
1	22 →	01-22
2	42 →	23-42
3	80 →	43-80
4	100 →	81-100

Customer 1: First random number is 14 - arrives after 1 minute
Second random number is 44 - time to be served 3 minutes

Customer 2: Random Number 73 - this is in the range 71-100 so he/she arrives after 3 minutes
Random number 87 - this is in the range 81-100 so he/she takes 4 minutes to be served

Assume only one checkout which opens at 9.00 am

Customer	Random number for arrival	Random number for service	Time between arrival	Time taken to be served	Arrives at	Served at	Leaves at	Customer wait before service (minutes)
1	14	44	1	3	9.01	9.01	9.04	0
2	73	87	3	4	9.04	9.04	9.08	0
3	46	70	2	3	9.06	9.08	9.11	2
4	53	02	2	1	9.08	9.11	9.12	3

From this firm can decide whether it thinks second checkout is needed; the situation with two checkouts can also be analysed using simulation analysis.

Reshaping in the 1990s

Restructuring (or 'reshaping'): reorganising of activities, e.g. downsizing, re-engineering and demerging.

Successful organisations are continually looking to reshape themselves to meet the changing needs of their environments to make themselves ever more competitive.

Diversification: moving into new and different business areas. This spreads risks but can be difficult to control.

Delayering: occurs when firms remove layers of management within their organisation structure.

Less layers should lead to:
- quicker decision making

- greater responsiveness to customer needs and wants

- greater responsibility (which can be motivating)

- less management costs

BUT
- individuals may lack training and ability

- individuals may suffer stress

Outsourcing: firms subcontract work out to independent suppliers rather than undertake the activities themselves. This allows firms to concentrate on their core activities and benefit from the expertise of specialists. For example, firms may subcontract their catering, their security, their office cleaning, market research or design work.

Downsizing: modern term for redundancy. Occurs when organisations attempt to increase their efficiency by reducing their staffing levels. Whilst this may reduce costs it can obviously cause uncertainty and fear amongst the employees who are left and resentment from those who are made redundant.

Re-engineering: "the fundamental rethinking and radical redesign of business processes to achieve dramatic improvements in critical, contemporary measures of performance such as cost, quality, service and speed." (M. Hammer and J. Champy). Re-engineering aims to improve business performance by organising work around a process rather than around tasks. When firms are trying to improve performance they tend to look at what they do at the moment and try to improve on this rather than thinking about whether there is a completely different way of serving the customer more effectively. Re-engineering occurs when managers ignore the way things are done at present and start with a blank piece of paper to create a new process. Re-engineering, therefore, involves radical and dramatic change.

Demerging: a firm splits itself up into separate, smaller business units. For example, ICI split into ICI and Zeneca, Hanson was divided into four separate companies and British Gas split into two parts.

Reasons:
- each business is able to respond independently to its own markets

- smaller units are easier to control and coordinate

BUT
- may lose economies of scale

- may lack as much market power

The trend in the past has been to get bigger; in recent years firms have tended to 'get back to basics' and focus on their core activities and split into smaller business units.

Success in the 1990s

To be successful in the 1990s firms need to:

Know the market
The key to competitive success lies in knowing what your customers want now and are likely to want in the future. Successful firms are proactive, i.e. they anticipate change rather than react to it.

Know the competition
Firms need to identify their areas of relative strength and weakness; they must monitor the market and measure their levels of cost and service against the competition.

Work with suppliers
The trend in the 1990s is not to select suppliers purely on the basis of price. It is important to consider other factors such as their quality, reliability and delivery schedules. Successful firms involve suppliers and develop a joint problem solving approach; they build long-term relationships with a few trusted suppliers - this is called 'partnership sourcing'.

Design products properly
A good design takes into account internal customers as well as external customers. A well designed product is relatively easy to make as well as satisfying customers' needs and wants.

Get it right and right again and right again
Production processes and the final goods and services must be reliable. Firms continually monitor their performance and develop ways of improving.

Flexible
Staff and equipment must be flexible to respond quickly to changing needs. This requires training and investment.

Put people together
Managers need to get people to share ideas and learn from each other. By bringing people together they are more likely to understand each others problems and find solutions.

Build a learning organisation
Managers need to encourage people to develop skills and to try out ideas even if they fail at first. People should be encouraged to be curious.

Time competitive
Increasingly firms are competing on time by producing products more quickly and delivering in a shorter time. Products can be developed more quickly by carrying out different parts of the process at the same time rather than waiting for one stage to finish before starting another, i.e. simultaneous engineering rather than a sequential approach. In 1981 Yamaha attacked Honda in the motor bike industry. Honda responded by rapid production development. In 1982 Honda had 60 models of motor bike; over the next 18 months it introduced or replaced 113 models.

Delight the customer
There are so many competitors that firms have to do more than satisfy the customer, they have to delight the customer. (This is Kwik Fit's stated aim). Successful organisations must not only meet customers expectations, they must surpass them. Shopping, for example, must be made a pleasant, interesting and enjoyable experience not a chore. This involves many factors such as: the products which are stocked, the decor of the shop, the aroma in the shop, the image of the store, the way in which customers are served, the way in which people can pay and the after sales service.

The successful organisation in the 1990s will:

- have a clear and shared view of where and how it will be successful (i.e. a mission)
- be able to predict change and respond quickly
- maintain the high levels of quality at an appropriate price
- learn faster than the competition

INDEX

Entries in **bold** type indicate main topic entries.